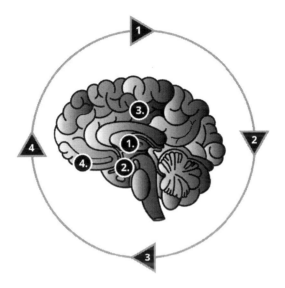

The Qortex Circuit

Train Your Brain for Joy and Transformation

Then Coach Anybody (Including Kids) to Do Anything

ED KANG

THE QORTEX CIRCUIT

Copyright © 2019 Ed Kang

All rights reserved.

ISBN: 9781696108225

DEDICATION

To Tae-Young, my wife, partner and BFF, and our two wonderous sons, Orlando and Julian.

THE QORTEX CIRCUIT

CONTENTS

| 01 | Introduction | 1 |
| 02 | The Problem with "How?" | 7 |

PART I: THE BRAIN SCIENCE OF JOY AND TRANSFORMATION

03	Blame It on the Brain	17
04	The "Courage 3-2-1" Technique	25
05	EQ for Transformation	35
06	Affective Neuroscience and Joy	41

PART II: FOUR STAGES OF THE QORTEX CIRCUIT

07	Stage 1: Attachment	47
08	Corrective Complex	55
09	Stage 2: Assessment	65
10	Metacognitive Reflection	75
11	Stage 3: Alignment	79
12	Collaborative Change Talks	87
13	Stage 4: Activation	99
14	Encouragement and Next Steps	107

APPENDIX A: QORTEX HACKS

APPENDIX B: QORTEX COACHING

THE QORTEX CIRCUIT

THE MISSION

To transform lives by making emotional health and mental performance coaching fun, fast and affordable for every child, parent, and leader in the world.

THE VISION

A transformed world where the next generation thrives because of this generation's leadership and joy.

@edkang99

THE QORTEX CIRCUIT

The information provided in this book is designed to provide helpful information on the subjects discussed. It is not intended to be used, and should not be used, as a substitute for legal counsel, medical evaluation, or for the diagnosis or treatment of any physical or mental health condition. Nor should the information be used as a substitute for consulting a licensed medical, mental health, legal, or other professional. A licensed physician, psychologist, and/or mental health provider should be consulted for diagnosis and treatment of any and all medical and mental health conditions. Call your physician or mental health professional or 911 for all emergencies. The publisher and author are not responsible for any specific medical or mental health needs that may require medical supervision and are not liable for any damages or negative consequences from any treatment, action, application, or preparation to any person reading or following the information in this book. References are provided for informational purposes only and do not constitute any endorsement of any websites or other sources. Readers should be aware that the websites listed in this book may change.

01
INTRODUCTION

The Qortex Circuit is a brain training framework for transformation based on the science of joy. Think of it as the OS (operating system) on any computer or mobile device. With the right OS, apps can be installed for pretty much anything. In the same way, the Qortex Circuit was designed to be an OS for your brain—powered by joy—to help you accomplish anything you've ever wanted.

Our brains are infinitely complex and powerful computers. The same way every computer has RAM (random access memory), the human brain has a short-term memory system. And just like a computer's hard drive, our brains also have long-term information storage capacity. The difference is the human brain can continually adapt and change its structure, where even the most advanced artificial intelligence cannot. But despite this powerful ability, without the right OS, powered by joy, the human brain is nowhere near as effective as it could be.

Which Comes First? Joy or Transformation?

We usually confuse joy and transformation, putting them in the wrong order. Unsurprisingly, we naturally assume that if we can transform our lives, we'll have more joy. This transformation could involve anything from getting in shape, finding that perfect job, falling in love, making enough money, or simply becoming our best selves in every area of life. We believe that if we can make certain changes, we'll have the health, wealth, wisdom, and relationships to truly enjoy our lives.

Unfortunately, transformation to achieve joy is not how our brains work. It's the other way around. You're about to learn that totally transforming your life requires training your brain for joy first. Your brain needs joy for any form of transformation.

Think of it in terms of weight loss. Many people try to lose weight because they want to get healthy. But medical experts will give you the opposite advice: You must get healthy to lose weight. What's the difference? Science has proven that when our bodies are healthy, and we consistently make healthy choices in alignment with how the systems of our bodies work, we naturally lose weight. It turns out that the *goal* of losing weight has nothing at all to do with actually losing weight.

Joy and transformation are no different than the scientific principles of weight loss. When we operate with joy, transformation happens naturally.

Joy at Work

Prioritizing joy first to achieve a desired transformation is the same advice I give to corporations. Many managers believe that if their employees would change their behaviors, they'd perform better and experience greater engagement at work. Once again, we've got this backward. If managers learn to engage their employees with joy *first*, performance and profit are virtually automatic.

Our brains require joy for optimal performance. Without joy, we become vulnerable to disengagement, isolation, and lack of emotional regulation. Without joy, we don't experience the psychological safety necessary to do our jobs with security and confidence. We don't take risks, can't be creative, and won't reach our full leadership potential.

Joy is a profit center and a competitive advantage for every business in any industry. Consider for a moment the brands that give us joy. Their products either give us joy by solving our problems, joyfully fulfilling our desires, or are delivered with great joy through the customer experience. What's the source of such joy? The answer, of course, is the people who lead the company and do the work.

Joy vs. Happiness

Another common misconception is our understanding of joy versus happiness. Happiness is important, but the problem with happiness is that it can place too much emphasis on how we feel about external circumstances beyond our control. Joy is an intrinsic and relational experience. By this I mean that we can experience joy regardless of external circumstances, and that true joy comes from being connected with other people. Our brains crave joyful connections as part of the human experience.

Joy is feeling glad to be with someone in times of strength and weakness. Joy makes us want to celebrate our victories together, but it also makes us grateful we have a shoulder to cry on during moments of defeat. By definition then, we don't necessarily have to feel happy to experience joy. In this way, joy helps us navigate challenges, build resilience, and achieve emotional maturity. Joy also supports our mental and physical health.

Joy for Transformative Coaching

The human brain is designed to experience joy right from the moment of birth. Our joyful experience starts with being held by parents and primary caregivers when we are at our weakest and most vulnerable. Joy is the reason we love holding babies and seeing them smile. There's no expectation for a baby to perform. We enjoy their presence and nothing more.

Beyond the initial love of a parent, the next best way to learn joy is through coaching. As soon as we begin to develop the skills and capacity to interact with the world, we experience coaching from multiple directions. While the term "coaching" is usually associated with athletics, there's a reason all these other forms of life coaching and executive coaching have exploded in popularity and demand. The right coaching, with joy, can accelerate our transformation.

The World Needs More Coaching

As our globalized economy flies at warp speed towards the future of work, coaching has become an increasingly vital performance skill. With technological advances towards automation and the scaling of today's management systems, those who've been coached by a "real" person, and can coach others the same way, have the advantage.

More importantly, coaching isn't limited to individuals with official titles and certifications (after a few courses, anybody can call themselves a coach anyway). Today, we can no longer solve problems with technical solutions alone. Challenges are now adaptive. And as the world becomes more volatile, uncertain, complex, and ambiguous (VUCA), anybody with leadership responsibilities can greatly benefit from the science of joy and art of coaching.

Manager-As-Coach

Coaching was once considered a luxury for an organization. But it's now a core skill, as managers are expected to develop teams, increase engagement, and get the most out of their people.

Parent-As-Coach

Raising children to have high self-esteem is not enough (it's also not working as intended). Children need different emotional support and practical coaching to navigate new multigenerational challenges.

Teacher-As-Coach

Teachers work alongside parents to prepare the next generation for future success. They help us learn and grow. But "learning to learn" requires more than academics. Today's student also needs coaching for social and emotional learning.

Consultant-As-Coach

Clients no longer want expert advice alone. Organizations today need support in aligning strategy and resources with execution and culture. A new hybrid consultant, where consulting and coaching come together, is becoming the standard organizations require.

Qortex Coaching

Once you learn the Qortex Circuit, you can use the power of joy to coach anybody to do anything for personal and professional transformation. How can such a grand and sweeping statement be made? The answer is we all use the same brain to do everything. Neuroscientists and psychologists are continually unlocking new insights on how to optimize the OS of our brains to realize human potential. This brain science can apply to coaching in any office, school, or even right at the kitchen table.

You don't have to be a neuroscientist or psychologist to take advantage of brain science. Today's scientists are more than happy to see their theories applied through practical and real-life experience. Professional practice and academic scholarship are always more effective when synergized. The world of brain science is no different.

This book takes a focused cross-section of current brain science and provides a practical everyday framework to help people experience joy, transform their lives, and then coach others to do the same. I hope it will inspire a lifelong journey of joy and transformation.

#ART: Appropriately Radical Transparency

In my desire to be authentic, individuals sometimes become uncomfortable with my levels of vulnerability. I've learned that true joy is accelerated by the courage to be vulnerable. But I admit I sometimes venture into TMI (too much information) territory and can be overly transparent. I'm continually learning and fine-tuning the art of appropriately radical transparency. At the same time, everybody's different. Some appreciate my brutal honesty while others bristle. So, I'll be marking certain sections with the hashtag #ART to flag any appropriately radical transparency. Feel free to scour, skim, or skip these sections as you like.

#EQ2iQ: How Does This Work for Children?

The brain doesn't fully develop until approximately 25 years old. While the principles of joy are the same before that time marker, a child's brain does not respond to Qortex coaching the same way an adult does. I'll be tagging this information with another hashtag, #EQ2iQ, to highlight the differences. EQ2iQ is the name of a specialized social and emotional learning program I developed to coach children and families.

02
THE PROBLEM WITH "HOW?"

Nobody denies the value of joy and transformation. Who doesn't want more joy, and who wouldn't want radical change for the better? The real question is "how?" We're bombarded every day with promises of health, wealth, and happiness. Gurus and social media influencers make things sound so easy. We're told to "just be yourself," "live, laugh, love," and "YOLO" (you only live once) through life.

If self-help and personal development were so easy, how do we explain that people seem to be getting more miserable every year? We can't ignore globally rising rates of obesity, adolescent depression, suicide, and opioid addiction. For some startling statistics, check out the latest World Happiness Report published by the United Nations (www.worldhappiness.report).

How many times have you tried some new self-help advice or a personal development program? And how many times have you achieved the results you expected? Or maybe the best question is, how many times have you found yourself in a cycle of disappointment after yet another failed attempt for change? If you're like the millions of people like me that keep the billion dollar self-help industry alive, then you don't like the honest answers to these questions. I know I don't.

#ART: My Weight Loss

Having struggled with my weight since marriage, I've tried every fad diet out there. From hormones to supplements, to even going vegan, I am the reigning champ of yo-yo dieting. I once lost 50 pounds only to gain it all back (plus another 15). I've exhausted myself countless times fighting my cravings and emotional eating. To this day, every time I see a "before and after" image anywhere, I grumble under my breath and reluctantly click on the video or post because, evidently, I enjoy torturing myself.

As a result, I've been fat-shamed everywhere from social media and clients in China (it's a cultural thing) to my mother. To put things in perspective, I was an amateur wrestler and martial artist in high school with the physique to match (another thing my mother reminds me of constantly). So nobody has been harder on me than me.

All this to say, I've had my share of "how?" questions. When it comes to weight loss, I know exactly what to do. But I didn't know how those who successfully transformed their bodies stuck to it. How did they overcome their habits? How did they maintain their results? How could I ever do the same?

Success Leaves Clues

As I've already introduced, being transformed has nothing to do with what we do, but whether we approach it with joy or not. Those who experience consistent joy in their lives do four things differently that automatically lead to transformation. I call them "transformation skills," and they are the following:

1. Develop appropriate attachments
2. Appropriately assess themselves and others
3. Appropriately align themselves and others
4. Activate their identities to lead others with joy

Not only do these individuals do things differently, but through transforming their mindsets, they think differently as well. They require no conscious effort when practicing these transformation skills. Their brains appear wired for automatic joy and continual transformation.

With closer examination, these four transformation skills provide clues to how you can train your brain for joy and transformation. Each skill activates and develops four different centers of the brain that can be considered an "experience-processing pathway." These interconnected parts of the brain make training faster than traditional learning (such as a taking a seminar or course), because training uses principles of brain science. This approach accelerates your brain's capacity for change.

How the Qortex Circuit Works

Through the rest of these chapters, I'm going to be introducing you to the Qortex Circuit and how it's used to accelerate brain training. The Qortex Circuit is broken down into four stages, representing the four transformation skills and four correlated centers of the brain.

Every individual has a Qortex Circuit. In the following chapter, I'll show you different ways for using it to train your brain using science and practical application exercises.

Here's a visual representation of the Qortex Circuit.

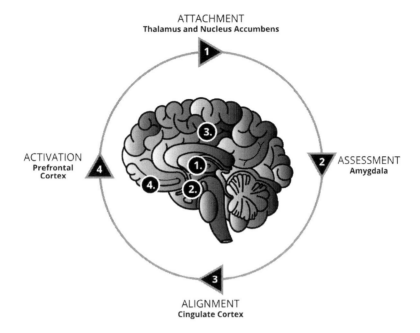

#ART: The Origin of the Qortex Circuit

Necessity is the mother of all invention. That's how I discovered the Qortex Circuit.

In 2018 I found myself at what seemed like a point of no return in Beijing, China. It was one of the darkest and most hopeless periods of my life. I'd moved to Beijing to launch an emotional intelligence startup developing training for organizations. But I struggled with isolation and growing mental health concerns. Although on the outside I appeared confident in the boardrooms of Fortune 500 companies, internally I was spiraling deeper into hopeless despair and unhealthy habits.

My sense of shame was painful; I knew I needed to change.. I watched countless YouTube videos and TED talks, and listened to popular podcasts for any hope. I tried to confide in my wife, but my pride and shame prevented me from being real with the struggle. Nothing was working.

Right when I was ready to pack it in and go home, I decided to revisit some research about emotional intelligence and the brain science of leadership. I started exploring the patterns of transformation skills that would eventually become the Qortex Circuit.

I saw the Qortex Circuit everywhere. I went back through my notes and had discussions with colleagues. The patterns got stronger. I devoured case studies and anecdotal evidence that reinforced my conclusions. I proposed theories to local neuroscientists and psychologists for more validation.

Then I tested the brain training. I started with small experiments using different techniques and iterated based on what I experienced. I was able to achieve results in my own life, and so I tried more experiments with clients. Today, the Qortex Circuit is the foundation for all my executive coaching and organizational consulting.

If not for my struggles, this work wouldn't exist. Reflecting on my experience I feel grateful. Yet there's a part of me that wishes I had gotten the help I needed much earlier. I won't take my mental health for granted again, and I hope anybody that reads this will do the same.

Based on Science and Practice

The Qortex Circuit integrates ongoing developments in neuroscience. Neuroscientists have discovered that skills for personal transformation and leadership are associated with different parts of the brain. In clinical psychology, this brain science is being used to address challenges in mental health. We can integrate this understanding to train our brains for improved mental performance.

Between coaching, workshops, and interviews, I've spent countless hours collecting evidence to support the Qortex Circuit. I'm beyond grateful to clients, colleagues, and my sons, Orlando and Julian, who've been gracious with their openness in this process. Here are a few stories that I hope inspire you as much as they inspired me.

Donald

Donald is an entrepreneur that suffered an unjust criminal conviction because of systemic corruption and lost his entire net worth. After being released from prison, he was forced to navigate a series of toxic relationships while being a single parent. But through perseverance and coaching, Donald is now building a multi-million-dollar business portfolio, enjoying healthy relationships, and watching his daughters thrive as youth athletes with scholarships.

Charity

Charity moved from the US to China and decided to change her life. She proceeded to lose 135 pounds and took her career development to a whole new level. Her commitment was as radical as her transformation. I remember spending many hours with her discussing her physical and mental approach to her weight loss goals. Recently I asked her to reflect on her journey, and her advice to me was profound. Charity's journey of physical, mental, and spiritual transformation has motivated me to do the same, and I can happily share that I'm the healthiest I've been in years.

Jason

Jason bounced from sales job to sales job because of a failed business and crushing personal debt. After taking responsibility and making some hard choices, he now runs a thriving training organization in China with government-level contracts. One story I distinctly remember was the time he became radically vulnerable, for the first time, with his wife. The result of that conversation still warms my heart when I think about it. Jason uses his emotional intelligence to help his daughter thrive socially, emotionally, and academically, despite the competitive pressures of the Chinese national education system. I enjoy spending time with him every time I am back in China.

Orlando

Orlando, at age 14, decided he wanted to be an entrepreneur. He started a skate camp during a summer break and earned enough to invest in a clothing and lifestyle brand. He now uses his business experience to earn credits towards high school. Orlando also happens to be my son, and, at the time of this writing, I'm his homeschool teacher.

KC

According to his bio, KC is a multi-talented composer, producer, musician, live performer, and DJ who is a master of his craft on and off the stage. His live shows are a combination of electric violin, keyboards, percussion, and mad energy. He also can be found producing and performing pop/dance, country, hip-hop, and world music, whether it's solo or in collaboration with other successful artists such as C+C Music Factory and Better Than Ezra. KC composes and creates full orchestral scores for TV, film, documentaries, and video games with major clients such as Budweiser. He has worked with the renowned radio station WKTU New York, and many other stations around the world.

As impressive as his bio may sound, I know KC best as a personal friend. He's been willing to help me refine anything I've concocted. So, I was excited to let him take the Qortex Circuit out for a test drive. Here's a letter from KC.

> Ed, your book *The Qortex Circuit* has become my missing link. I am very big on books with the purpose of improving my business and me personally. Books like *Awaken The Giant*, *The One Thing* and my absolute favorite book, *Essentialism* by Greg McKeown. These books provide invaluable ways of conducting business, state changes, constant energy, and motivation. All of which should be life-changing. For some reason, however, I could not

understand why I wasn't getting the lasting change and results others were. And why I could read these books over and over, memorize what they said, yet somehow I could not build the anchors in my brain to create a steadfast foundation for me or my business.

As I started reading *The Qortex Circuit* and tried the corresponding exercises at the end of each chapter, something odd happened. And then it happened again. And again, and again. Not only did I start experiencing "Aha!" moments, but I also started to see my foundation get stronger and unmovable. Game-changing and life-altering would be an understatement. I have experienced amazing state changes, motivation, and excitement for moving forward in my life. If I had to sum this book up in one phrase, it would be "Bridging Your Gap To Greatness." The only thing that excites me more than watching the effect this book will have on my business, personal life, and the people around me, is trying to guess just how many languages and how many bestseller lists this book will join around the world.

PART I
THE BRAIN SCIENCE OF JOY AND TRANSFORMATION

@EDKANG99

03
BLAME IT ON THE BRAIN

Saying the human brain has a "mind of its own" may seem strange, even a little ridiculous, but it's not far from the truth. That three-pound wrinkly mass between our ears is responsible for everything from breathing to dreams, emotions, memory, and shaping our humanity. And most of the time, we're not even conscious of how it's all happening.

Tom Bilyeu, cofounder of Quest Nutrition, a protein and health products company recently acquired for $1 billion, posted the following on his YouTube channel *Impact Theory*:

> If you don't understand the biological realities of the brain, you'll never understand the mind. If you don't understand the mind, you'll forever remain its servant rather than the other way around.

The easiest way to approach the brain is to think of it as a system. The brain has a set of principles and procedures that work together to get things done. Anybody can then take a systematic approach to brain training, which is the purpose of the Qortex Circuit.

There are two biological realities we must first understand: efficacy and efficiency. These are two operating principles that can work for us or against us. Let's start with efficacy first.

Blame It on Chinese Food

Efficacy is the ability to produce a desired or intended result. We all want and need efficacy in our lives. But this is where the problem begins when it comes to self-help and personal development.

Efficacy is to self-help what monosodium glutamate (MSG) is to Chinese food. MSG is a flavor enhancer. And while the Food and Drug Administration says it's generally a safe food ingredient, ongoing complaints about the negative effects of MSG have been piling up for years. Regardless of its reputation in the west, however, MSG continues to make Chinese food taste delicious. Billions of people who eat Chinese food, in China and around the world, consume MSG daily.

You can find MSG in all sorts of food products because of its flavor. Food that tastes delicious activates the pleasure centers of the brain. Therefore, food is a drug and different forms of it can be just as addictive as other substances. In the same way, efficacy is the flavor enhancer that's added to the entire self-help industry. Efficacy is how every self-help guru enhances the belief that their program will work, just for you, regardless of how many others you've tried.

Efficacy creates confidence that all goals and desires are achievable. Gurus promise that anything is possible—if you're willing to invest in their programs of course. Every popular self-help text on the planet relies on efficacy, sprinkled with various doses of practical advice. It's a tried-and-true formula that works because we all want to be the hero in our own stories.

The problem is the brain resists efficacy. To be more specific, our brains resist the changes involved with efficacy. As infinitely complex as it is, the human brain is designed to take the path of least resistance. In other words, the brain will always try to choose *efficiency* over *efficacy*.

Blame It on Neuroplasticity

Neuroplasticity is the brain's ability to form synaptic connections in response to experiences, such as learning. According to Brazilian researcher Dr. Suzana Herculano-Houzel, there are approximately 86 billion neurons in your brain that connect to transmit signals.

Neuroscientists will tell you, "neurons that fire together wire together," which is how neural pathways form. For example, learning to drive requires initial instruction and experience. At first, driving is a foreign experience, feeling quite unnatural. But after a while, it becomes second nature because new neural pathways turn new driving skills into old habits.

On the one hand, the upside of neuroplasticity is that anything we learn to do, with enough repetition, will become an automatic habit. On the other hand, our brains can get stuck in autopilot.

How many times have you driven to a destination without really remembering how you got there? One time after moving to a new home, I drove to my old house after work every day for a week. I was so conditioned to drive the same roads that while preoccupied with other thoughts, I automatically took the familiar route without a second thought. To this day, my wife will tell you that my brain has a mind of its own when I'm behind the wheel.

To maximize the brain's efficiency, it will switch to autopilot and automatically follow habits hardwired through experience and repetition. For every positive habit trained into our brains, not-so-positive habits can potentially get programmed the same way (neuroplasticity doesn't discriminate). So when it comes to changing habits, our brains will put up a fight to stick with their pre-established and efficient neural pathways.

It's a misconception that people don't like change. We all want to change, especially if that change is considered positive. And most of the time, we know what to do for the desired change. But we don't do it. Not because we have bad attitudes (not at first anyway), but because our brains get overwhelmed and are designed to protect us. The brain does this by making change seem painful.

Blame It on the Prefrontal Cortex and Amygdala

Brain scientists have observed that the basal ganglia control daily activities like driving home from work every day. This part of the brain manages repetitive tasks and ensures it doesn't expend any more mental energy than necessary to perform routine activities.

The basal ganglia will default to "the way it's always been done." It's a mode that keeps our systems in homeostasis (stable equilibrium), which creates mental comfort. The comfort of homeostasis feels good, and our brains want to keep it that way.

When confronted with change, our prefrontal cortex is engaged. The prefrontal cortex handles executive functions such as insight, self-control, and personality expression. And the prefrontal cortex is linked to the amygdala, which is the part of our brains responsible for the stress response ("fight or flight").

Attempting transformation requires challenging our routines and comfort zones. This disruption sends new information to the prefrontal cortex, which can be overwhelming. But because the prefrontal cortex is connected, the amygdala is then triggered, sending us into fight-or-flight mode. The brain is processing something that is out of homeostasis and attempts to restore systems to normal. And this interaction can cause psychological and even physical pain.

Emotionally, this typically starts as anger, disgust, or fear. But if unresolved, we start to feel sadness, despair, and ultimately shame.

Blame It on Repetition and Negativity

Gandhi once said, "A man is but the product of his thoughts. What he thinks, he becomes." And as the ancient proverb goes, "As a man thinketh in his heart, so is he." In summary, you are what you think.

According to the National Science Foundation, the average person has between 12,000 and 60,000 thoughts per day. Of those thoughts, 95% are repetitive, with a staggering 80% being negative.

Individuals that struggle with addiction share that most of their daily thoughts are indeed repetitive and negative. The majority of their thoughts also relate to their addiction. Those that struggle with obesity will attest to thinking about food all day. Drug addicts and alcoholics experience the same. This pattern also applies to digital addictions like social media. The number of times people check their notifications, especially first thing in the morning, is one of the signs.

Beyond addictions, workplace stress is equally serious. If we work every day, thinking about how much we hate our jobs or fear the boss, our bodies will react accordingly. The byproduct of these repetitive thought patterns is chronic stress, which can lead to depression and anxiety. A recent study led by the World Health Organization estimated that depression and anxiety disorders cost the global economy a trillion dollars in annual lost productivity.

Other conditions, such as loneliness and social isolation, have reached epidemic levels. The UK appointed the first Minister for Loneliness in 2018. And the American Association of Retired Persons reports that prolonged isolation can be as lethal as smoking 15 cigarettes a day. The fact is, our bodies aren't designed to be under such a constant state of stress. We become vulnerable, degrading the body's natural immune systems, putting us at risk of disease and other conditions.

Blame It on White Matter

When describing the brain, we tend to picture it being made up of gray matter. But there's also something called white matter that makes up 60% of our cerebrums. White matter is where the brain stores habits. White matter also runs up to 200 times faster than gray matter.

Your brain updates its state multiple times every second. Think of it like the refresh rate on a digital screen, which is how fast images are updated. During conscious left-brain-dominant activities, such as solving problems and processing language, your brain updates its state five times per second (5 Hz). Right-brain-dominant activities, like motivation and caring for others, update brain states at six times per second (6 Hz). But these are gray matter speeds. They don't compare to the speed of habits stored in white matter.

Habits are prepackaged responses to known situations. When specific response repeat, neurons wire together to form a neural pathway for the habit. That's when the white matter goes into action. Over the month or so it takes to form a habit, white matter wraps and insulates the habit pathway. This insulation allows electrical signals to jump from neuron to neuron, increasing transmission speeds of the nerve signals. As a result, that habit pathway will fire 200 times faster than if it were just made up of gray matter alone.

White matter means that the more we practice transformation skills, the more natural they'll become, until they're seemingly automatic. We can act with no extra conscious deliberation. For all this to occur, however, your brain requires some form of disruption to first change behaviors. Next, the new behaviors need enough repetition to form habits that become insulated by white matter.

To quote late author and motivational speaker Zig Ziglar, "Your input determines your outlook. Your outlook determines your output, and your output determines your future." This gem perfectly describes Qortex coaching and everything I'm going to be asking you to do next.

Brain Training Exercise

From this point on, you're going to need a journal. If you don't have one, get one. But it should be a paper journal for writing. Sorry, no typing on your phone or tablet.

There are well-documented benefits of writing by hand in a physical journal. The act of writing stimulates focus and learning. First, you won't be distracted by notifications. Second, your senses be overstimulated with artificial light and frequencies. And third, writing by hand activates a part of your brain called the Reticular Activating System (RAS). The RAS prioritizes anything that requires immediate focus and filters out distractions. Thus, activating the RAS will help process and accelerate what you're learning.

Qortex Coaching Assignment

Once you have a journal, write down three names of people you plan to coach first. Setting this intention will motivate you to retain and apply everything you learn. In later chapters, I'll show you how to coach others using the Qortex Circuit. This assignment is meant to get you started.

@EDKANG99

04
THE "COURAGE 3-2-1" TECHNIQUE

There's a method to "tricking" the brain for transformation and bypassing any hardwired resistance. It involves training the body's nervous systems to regulate the stress response that fights change. It's a method that disrupts old patterns, priming the brain for new inputs.

The method is a breathing and meditation exercise I call the "Courage 3-2-1" technique. Think of it as a boot camp for your brain. It takes less than ten minutes, and you'll experience changes immediately. I'm going to ask you to do it daily. It's also a coaching exercise you can quickly teach others.

First, I'd like to give some credit where it's due regarding the origins of "Courage 3-2-1".

Wim Hof

Wim "The Iceman" Hof is a Dutch extreme athlete who's held Guinness World Records for swimming under ice, prolonged full-body contact with ice, and a barefoot half-marathon on ice and snow. Although he sounds like a superhero, Hof achieved these remarkable feats using the Wim Hof Method (WHM), a form of breathing and meditation training he developed.

WHM claims to improve sleep, willpower, sports performance, stress, creativity, and immune systems, along with a host of other benefits. Many note that WHM has similarities to Tibetan Tummo meditation and the practice of pranayama, which also employs breathing and meditation techniques. Regardless, WHM practitioners attest to the positive effects of WHM.

Mel Robbins

Mel Robbins is a television host, author, and motivational speaker. She's renowned for her TEDx talk "How to Stop Screwing Yourself Over" and best-selling book *The 5 Second Rule*. "The 5 Second Rule" is a metacognition technique (thinking about thinking). It involves counting down from five, trusting your instincts, and then acting on a goal.

Robbins teaches "The 5 Second Rule" as a way of tricking your brain into achieving your greater goals. It involves cultivating what's known as an "internal locus of control," which means believing you have control over your outcomes and future success. In the book *Happiness Advantage: The Seven Principles that Fuel Success and Performance at Work* by Shawn Achor, this concept is called the "Zorro Circle". Achor also gave his own popular TED talk. Research shows that those with an internal locus of control are happier, in better health, more likely to succeed at work, and have lower levels of anxiety and depression.

After discovering Hof and Robbins, I experimented with WHM and "The 5 Second Rule". Immediately, I recognized their effects on the same centers of the brain featured in the Qortex Circuit. Diving into the research cited by Hof and Robbins validated my assumptions. And after months of trying various iterations, I added emotional intelligence and neurolinguistic programming (NLP) to my version. My objective was to create a single technique that would be as effective as WHM and "The 5 Second Rule" combined. But it also needed to be efficient enough to minimize the brain's resistance to change. The result was the "Courage 3-2-1" technique, which I've been teaching in workshops and to executive coaching clients ever since.

To test the "Courage 3-2-1" technique, I spent 40 days doing nothing else. I did it in the shower every morning (still do). I found my self-awareness improving without having to think about it consciously. Then I tried integrating exercises such as prayer, stretching, and journaling, to see how their effects worked in combination. Every extra technique came more naturally and required less willpower to maintain as a consistent practice.

The most profound effect I experienced was increased self-regulation. I became more emotionally centered and enjoyed greater impulse control. I improved in every facet as a leader; again, without spending extra conscious energy trying to do so.

At times, I wondered if the results were unique to me or too good to be true. But clients who tried it for their very first time reported similar results. They shared an immediate sense of inner calm and stress reduction. In workshops, participants overcame their fear of public speaking. They also gained the courage to authentically share emotional needs and give candid feedback to their peers.

Technique Overview

The central premise of the "Courage 3-2-1" technique involves combining breathing, meditation, and metacognition techniques to reset the brain and prime it for disruption (changing inputs to shift the outlook). On the most basic level, this starts with deep breathing, almost intentionally hyperventilating to get enough oxygen to your body and brain. It's designed to increase mindfulness and create an internal locus of control. You'll also repeat emotional vocabulary to train your brain for emotional intelligence.

Give the "Courage 3-2-1" technique a try when you're ready.

Find a comfortable spot. You're going to be speaking out loud, so it's probably best to be alone in case others might overhear and potentially make you self-conscious. Read these instructions and practice each step on its own. Once you memorize the process and get the hang of it, you can put it all together.

Step 1: Take deep breaths in and out.

Breathe in through the nose and out through the mouth like a straw. Breathe slowly and intentionally. Expand your chest and let the air fill your lungs. But don't breathe out like you're blowing on a campfire or at candles on a cake. Just let the air escape through your mouth by collapsing your diaphragm. Breathe as deeply as possible, maximizing each breath. You'll be on the verge of hyperventilating. Keep doing this until feeling a slight tingle in your lips or a light-headed buzz.

Step 2: Repeat the emotion statements.

After enough deep breaths, continue to breathe in and out, repeating the following statements at the bottom of each breath. Say them one at a time, with each breath, in the following order:

1. "I feel courage."
2. "I feel trust."
3. "I feel optimism."
4. "I feel acceptance."
5. "I feel understanding."
6. "I feel love."
7. "I feel joy."
8. "I feel peace."

Step 3: Hold at the bottom of a breath.

Take a deep breath and fill your lungs. Then breathe out, emptying them. Then hold your breath at the bottom as long as you possibly can. Pretend like you're having an underwater breath-holding contest in a pool. You'll feel your body go into a panic. That's how long you should try to hold your breath.

Step 4: Hold at the top of a breath.

When you can't hold any longer, take a deep breath in (it'll be more like a gasp) and hold it at the top for 20-30 seconds before letting it out. You'll feel a rush of relief, even a bit of euphoria.

Step 5: Keep breathing normally.

Take a few more breaths to settle down.

Step 6: Say, "I feel courage 3-2-1," then snap your fingers.

Say, "I feel courage," then count down from three to one and snap your fingers. If you don't know how to snap, this is a great reason to learn.

That's it. If you haven't yet tried it, schedule a time before the next chapter.

Technique Tips

When breathing in, pay attention to expanding your chest, straightening your back, and lifting your shoulders. Breathe out into your stomach, extending your belly. Focus on your breath and how it feels through your nose and mouth. Doing this will prevent your mind from wandering.

The emotions in the technique are in a very specific order. I've based the list upon the research of human vibratory frequencies. All objects and organisms on the planet vibrate at different frequencies. These frequencies can be measured down to the cellular level.

Every emotion vibrates at a different frequency. And since all vibrations emit energy, we can have high-energy emotions and low-energy emotions that affect our brains and bodies differently. The order of the emotions is designed to tune our bodies to higher-energy frequencies. Think of it like turning up a dial one frequency at a time.

Be sure to use the words "I feel" when practicing the emotion statements. Saying "I feel" practices emotional intelligence. It develops mindfulness through being intentionally present by using the appropriate tense. Repeating the emotions also builds stronger neural pathways in the brain for emotional agility.

If you would like to use personal affirmations, add them at the end of the technique. Feel free also to add any other practices based on your spiritual beliefs.

Holding your breath is designed to trigger the body's stress response and release adrenaline. It will help kick-start the brain and reset various hormones.

After holding your breath and releasing it, you'll feel a rush of relief. It's a signal from your brain that your systems are returning to a state of homeostasis. Cognitively, you're learning to regulate the fight-or-flight response. By causing your body to panic, you also build the mental capacity to respond appropriately in other stressful situations. This practice is a way to build psychological resilience.

As you practice the technique, stay in the moment. Pay attention to the shape of your body and how it feels. Focus on your breath and how it feels on your lips and lungs. It will clear your mind and help you practice mindfulness.

Use It All Day Any Time

I was inspired to add a snap by John, my friend and colleague in China. While working together, I'd notice John snap his fingers loudly at various points during the day. He explained it was a way to "send a sound to my mind and a strong movement to my body." For John, this was to release pressure and manage personal energy, aligning mind and body. At first, I imitated his snapping to poke fun. But after a few times, I noticed a similar positive reaction. Fascinated, I continued to experiment.

When feeling stressed, overwhelmed, or triggered, say, "I feel courage 3-2-1," and snap your fingers. Then immediately move forward with whatever task is immediately required. I do this right before getting on stage when speaking. I've also done it before important meetings, especially when there was an expected confrontation. And whenever I get bad news, such as a surprise bill or a negative notification, this technique has helped me respond appropriately versus reacting emotionally.

Use It with Cold Showers

Try combining the "Courage 3-2-1" technique with a cold shower. Start with the water running at your preferred temperature and do the technique. Then after snapping your fingers, immediately turn the hot water to cold and stay there until you can't take it anymore. It will introduce a new level of brain disruption and will mentally energize you. There are other benefits to cold exposure for your immune system and psychological resilience. Feel free to research this for yourself.

Brain Training Exercise

Copy the "Courage 3-2-1" instructions into your journal. Writing them down will help with memorization. While referencing it, like a manual, the journal will also be available to record any thoughts and reflections that come to mind.

Practice the "Courage 3-2-1" technique every day as you work through this book. Mornings are typically best. You could also use this book as a reminder. Every time you pick it up, do the technique before reading.

Qortex Coaching Application

Remember those three names you wrote down in the last chapter? Pick one and teach them the "Courage 3-2-1" technique when you're ready. Coach them verbally through each step. Then ask them what they noticed and how they feel.

#EQ2iQ: Courage and Breathing for Children

From birth to approximately three years of age, a healthy child learns how to experience and receive joy without guilt or fear. They achieve this by bonding and learning trust with adults. Starting from age three, children can learn persistence and doing hard things, introducing them to the concept of courage. And the more adults are willing to discuss and model courage with children, the more children develop mental fortitude and resilience.

To do this, start by teaching the child courageous self-talk. Teach the child to say, "I am brave," "I will be brave," and "I can be brave." Next, ask the child to combine them to say, "I am. I will. I can." Consistently practice this with them in all situations, especially when they're afraid.

Next, teach the child deep breathing. It will train them in self-regulation and calm during emotional moments. Have the child lie on their back and place their hand on their chest and stomach. Place your hand on top of theirs. Tell them to make their hand rise with their chest while breathing in, and then the same with their stomach while breathing out. Later, as needed, recall the exercise by saying, "Remember the chest and stomach breathing exercise? Let's do that right now." You can also teach this by using a feather in your palm or dangling a strip of paper in front of their mouth.

It's fun teaching a child to snap their fingers so they can eventually practice the full "Courage 3-2-1" technique. By doing this, you'll reinforce bonds of joy and trust.

A word of caution. When teaching a child to do hard things, don't utilize a strict "no quitting" policy. It can lead to problems with performance anxiety by attaching guilt and shame to quitting. Instead, teach a child to process their options and choose the most courageous path they're mature enough to take. If they still choose to quit, celebrate the emotional process. Help them learn that sometimes, the most courageous acts require making hard choices in the face of emotional pressure.

@EDKANG99

05
EQ FOR TRANSFORMATION

EQ stands for "emotional quotient." EQ has been popular since 1995 with the publication of the international bestseller *Emotional Intelligence, Why It Can Matter More Than IQ*, by Daniel Goleman.

According to TalentSmart, one of the world's leading emotional intelligence training organizations, individuals with high EQ earn an average of $29,000 more per year compared to their lower EQ counterparts. They've also found that 90% of top performers have high EQ, and EQ is responsible for 58% of job performance.

EQ is the foundation for transformation. Making an additional $29,000 every year is considered a positive change for most of us. For many, however, that amount of money can be transformational. What could you do with an extra $29,000 in the bank every year?

Traditionally, being a high performer—while getting compensated accordingly—was attributed to a high IQ. We've now learned that high performance in any area of life is not just what you do, but also how you do it. For example, your technical skills (IQ) may help you get a job, but it's your interpersonal skills such as communication and leadership, which are all EQ-based, that help you keep your job and get promoted.

EQ and the Future of Work

According to the Future of Jobs Report published in 2018 by the World Economic Forum, the top ten growing skills for work by 2022 are

1. Analytical thinking and innovation
2. Active learning and learning strategies
3. Creativity, originality, and initiative
4. Technology design and programming
5. Critical thinking and analysis
6. Complex problem-solving
7. Leadership and social influence
8. Emotional intelligence
9. Reasoning, problem-solving, and ideation
10. Systems analysis and evaluation

Although emotional intelligence is eighth on the list, I argue that EQ is critical to every other skill listed, especially considering that most work today is done in teams. Teams with a higher collective EQ consistently perform better.

What EQ Is and What It Is Not

Emotional intelligence, as the name implies, is the ability to be intelligent about emotions. The more intelligent you are about your emotions, the better you can manage them and respond appropriately. You can also help others do the same. As the term "emotional quotient" implies, emotional intelligence is a measure of how much you know about your emotions and the practical skills to manage yourself, and others, concerning those emotions.

EQ is not a measure of your moral character, which is a common misconception. We tend to accuse people of having low EQ because they lack compassion or integrity. But the reality is it's possible to be morally corrupt and still possess high emotional intelligence. EQ is a skill that anybody can practice and master regardless of character. Taken to extremes, an individual can be emotionally intelligent and even a narcissist at the same time.

For the above reason, it's not enough to develop EQ alone. In conjunction with emotional intelligence, we should be seeking to develop emotional agility, emotional responsibility, and emotional maturity. These are the four cornerstones that are critical to be an effective Qortex Coach. And the best way to understand each is to ask "what," "when," "how," and "who."

Emotional Intelligence—the "What"

As introduced, EQ is how intelligent we are about emotions. EQ helps us answer the question, "What am I feeling?" Therefore EQ starts with the skill of self-awareness. Self-awareness is foundational for other EQ skills like self-regulation, motivation, empathy, and social skills.

Emotional Agility—the "When"

Emotional agility is the ability to accurately identify patterns of emotions and the appropriate timing for a response. Emotional agility lets us answer the questions, "When do I feel this way?", and "When should I respond?" Without emotional agility, we experience something called "emotional amplification," which intensifies unresolved emotions and results in "emotional leakage." Emotional leakage occurs when we can no longer contain unresolved emotions, and allow our feelings to affect others around us inappropriately.

Emotional Responsibility—the "How"

Emotional responsibility asks the questions, "How did I get here?", and then "How can I take responsibility?" With the right answers, we can take emotional responsibility for past actions and determine how to respond in the present situation appropriately. Taking responsibility prevents us from falling into a victim mentality and creates opportunities to develop resilience. We can also take responsibility for our feelings without taking responsibility for how others feel. In this, responsibility is distinctly different from accountability. Accountability is fear-based while emotional responsibility can be taken with joy.

Emotional Maturity—the "Who"

The ultimate objective of Qortex coaching is emotional maturity. While we can be responsible for ourselves, maturity means we're willing also to be responsible for the well-being and development of others. When we're operating with emotional responsibility, we're able to ask and answer the following questions:

- "Who am I?"
- "Who do I want to be?"
- "Whom do I want to be me with?"

The answers to these "who" questions focus our sense of identity and belonging, which translates into the highest levels of executive function in the brain. All the most inspiring and influential leaders function at high levels of emotional maturity and can tell you, with confidence and clarity, who they are, who they want to be, and whom they want to be themselves with.

#EQ2iQ: EQ Skills Are like Any Other Subject

Since the industrial age, the education system has always emphasized technical subjects such as math and science. This trend is now changing. Organizations such as the World Economic Forum warn us of the new skills required in the workforce because of the advancement of robots, AI, and automation. Yet currently there remains a traditional educational paradigm around how to help children succeed in the future of work.

EQ skills are as critical as any other core subject. If high grades in math are required to become an accountant, shouldn't EQ-based skills, such as conflict management, be treated with the same importance for corporate managers? As organizations are currently complaining that students aren't graduating with the necessary people skills for today's challenges, shouldn't the education industry respond accordingly?

Even a small but consistent focus on EQ in the classroom can help students go further in academics. According to a study by the non-profit group Six Seconds, when a group of students learned EQ one class per week, traditional math lessons were easier to teach compared to the classes that didn't receive EQ instruction. After three months, the teacher noted that not only did the students improve math learning but improved relationships, communication, and problem-solving in the classroom as well.

My sincere hope is that parents and teachers reframe the formal role of EQ in education. Although approaches such as social-emotional learning are gaining prominence, they're still not considered core components to the academic journey. We owe it to our children, and future generations that will inherit this earth, to reconsider our approach.

@EDKANG99

06
AFFECTIVE NEUROSCIENCE AND JOY

Affective neuroscience is the study of the neural mechanisms of emotion. It's also considered an interdisciplinary field that combines neuroscience with the psychological study of personality, emotion, and mood.

Dr. Allan Schore, from UCLA, is often introduced as the "Einstein of psychoanalysis." One of Schore's recognized achievements was taking different fields of research and unifying them into a coherent model of the brain. In his book, *Affect Regulation and the Origin of the Self: The Neurobiology of Emotional Development,* Schore writes extensively on how the brain works while referencing key research on how the brain learns through the emotion of joy.

Joy

Joy is the renewable resource that powers all Qortex coaching. Joy is different than happiness. Happiness is associated with your external circumstances. Joy is the feeling of being glad to be with someone not only in our celebrated strengths, but especially in our vulnerable weaknesses. Joy is a relational experience. It's the sparkle in our eye when we see those that delight us. Joy gives us the peace to share our deepest shame and bond with others that protect us. Therefore, we don't have to feel happy or excited to have joy.

Joy strengthens loving relationships. We love people as a response to joy, not the other way around. Joy creates a high-energy state in the brain. It helps us process suffering and pain while maintaining connections with the people we love. Joy allows us to be resilient and productive with others, even in the hardest times.

According to the work of Dr. Allan Schore and others such as Dr. Antonio Damasio and Dr. Karl Lehman, we all have an "experience-processing pathway." This pathway starts at the bottom of the right brain and works its way through four major centers. It ends at the "joy center" in the right orbital prefrontal cortex, which is the center that has executive control over our entire emotional system. When this center is fully developed, we more effectively regulate emotions and control pain. It even boosts our immune system. It's also the only part of the brain that can override main drive centers of food and sexual impulses, and the emotions of terror and rage.

Your joy center is the only section of your brain that never loses its capacity to grow. We can continually train the joy center for the rest of our lives. The implications are that no matter what age, with the right joyful relationships in our lives, we can grow and even repair our capacity for emotional intelligence, agility, responsibility, and maturity—all thanks to joy.

Team Qortex

Imagine a relay race team with four runners on a circular track. Let's call them Team Qortex. Each runner represents a different stage of the Qortex Circuit and passes a "joy baton" to the next runner. The faster each runner smoothly hands off the joy baton, the more Team Qortex wins. But this race never ends. After stage four of the Qortex Circuit, the runner passes the joy baton to the runner at stage one for another lap. And again, because of joy, Team Qortex never runs out of energy.

Team Qortex needs coaching. Just like any relay race, Team Qortex can get "stuck" at different stages of the Qortex Circuit. The runners can stumble and drop the baton during hand-offs. They can even completely stop running or get confused and run in the wrong direction. And in some cases, the track could be shut down, preventing any running at all.

The track of the Qortex Circuit represents the experience-processing pathway. Think of each runner as a different center of our brains. When the brain's capacity is strong and healthy, the runners zip around the track passing the joy baton with ease. In this optimal state, transformation skills are practiced automatically without conscious thought. Speed is the sign that white matter has insulated the neural pathways for accelerated performance.

In a brain that lacks transformation skills and habits, the experience-processing pathway can become cramped, and even shut off in certain centers. One of the causes is when the runners carry a fear baton instead of the joy baton. When motivated by fear, we become out of touch with ourselves and the world around us. We become reactive, rigid, and, worst of all, self-righteous. Another way to describe this state is being "relationally offline."

#ART: My Team Qortex Story

I can't remember anything about my childhood and growing up in a family. My mind is completely blank up to about age eleven. I can't picture my homes or describe my parents. I have small fragments of joyful experiences with my father, like learning to fish and skating, but when it comes to my mother, there's a void. Looking at family pictures from the past is like watching a documentary for the first time.

I do vividly remember my friends' families and homes. I can recall the meals they prepared and the activities we shared. I even remember their pets. Sadly, I've always related to my friends' mothers more than my own.

I used to chalk this up to bad memory. But all would be shattered during a family BBQ one summer.

While sitting by the firepit, my brother Eric revealed that I suffered abuse as a child. He recounted memories of traumatic events he witnessed and endured. At first, it was hard to believe. To me, my parents were my elders, whom I honored the best I could. But as Eric continued to share, the reasons for my "bad" memory started to make sense.

After spending some time confused and disillusioned, I learned through executive coaching and counseling that childhood trauma had shut off certain parts of my brain. Painful memories were repressed, and my experience-processing pathway was shut down in certain areas. It all explained my specific behaviors as a young adult that verged on having an anti-social personality disorder. My brain also lacked any capacity for emotional empathy. Combined, I often joke that I was a dysfunctional mess with the emotional intelligence of a chair (it was that bad). I was insufferable, especially for my wife, during the first decade of marriage.

While sad, I know I'm not alone in this experience.

I've met others that can relate to my story. They recognize their Qortex Circuits are stuck or shut down. Helping others is the reason Qortex coaching gets me excited. We can retrain our brains and reactivate the Qortex Circuit. Our brains can function with joy. And vulnerability and courage make this process even faster.

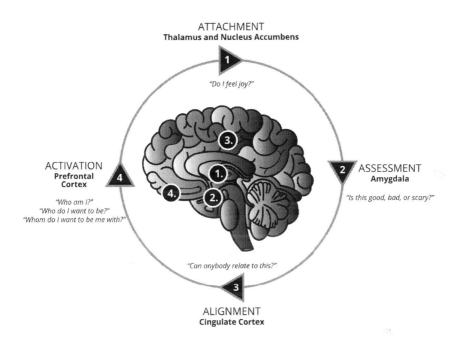

PART II
FOUR STAGES OF THE QORTEX CIRCUIT

@EDKANG99

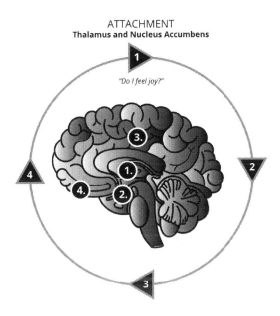

07
STAGE 1: ATTACHMENT
DEVELOPING APPROPRIATE ATTACHMENTS

Attachment theory is a psychological model for understanding how we form and respond to relationships, especially when hurt, separated from loved ones, or perceiving a threat. Attachment theory suggests that all children need to bond with at least one parent (ideally two) for healthy social and emotional development.

We learn attachment the moment we're born. As we explore relationships, we learn attachment patterns throughout childhood that affect how we as adults relate to our partners, children, and peers.

These patterns determine how we

- Respond to emotional intimacy in relationships
- Communicate and fill our emotional needs
- Empathize and fill the emotional needs of others
- Respond to relational conflict
- Manage expectations of ourselves and others

Joy plays a critical role in attachment. The more joy we experience, the healthier our attachments become. This is the reason that, in stage one of the Qortex Circuit, our brains ask, "Do I feel joy?"

Thalamus and Nucleus Accumbens

Attachment in the brain starts with the thalamus and nucleus accumbens. This center is where the brain's experience-processing pathway begins.

Your thalamus, located just above the brain stem, is responsible for relaying sensory signals, including motor signals, to the rest of the brain. It regulates consciousness, sleep, and alertness. Recent research suggests that the thalamus also contributes to cognitive flexibility by wiring different circuits of the brain together to help make complex decisions.

The nucleus accumbens is part of the brain's reward system. It's also referred to as the pleasure center. Its operation works with two neurotransmitters: dopamine and serotonin.

Dopamine motivates us to see rewards and take actions towards them. Dopamine contributes to feelings of satisfaction and motivation. It's released during pleasurable situations and stimulates us to seek out rewarding activities such as learning and novelty—food, sex, gambling, and drugs all trigger dopamine release. So, as part of the reward system, it also plays a part in addiction.

Serotonin is known as the "happy hormone." It's thought to regulate mood and social behavior, appetite and digestion, sleep, memory, and sexual desire and function. Serotonin helps override immediate impulses to achieve long-term and abstract goals versus short-term rewards. Studies also have found links between low serotonin levels and depression.

Appropriate and Inappropriate Attachment

Psychologists identify four "attachment styles." We can have secure, anxious, avoidant, and disorganized attachment styles. I prefer to simplify it to appropriate and inappropriate attachments.

Appropriate attachments are joy-based and create secure bonds with others. Through joy-based attachments, we can enjoy secure relationships with emotional intimacy. We allow ourselves to depend on others and allow them to depend on us without creating codependency. We're also empathetic, trusting, tolerant, and forgiving of past issues and hurts.

Another indicator of appropriate attachment is "reciprocal autonomy." Reciprocal autonomy is when each person in the relationship accepts the other's need for separateness without feeling threatened, rejected, or jealous. There's a mutual respect that creates a psychological balance between autonomy and relatedness, which is the social nature of human beings and the need to relate to others.

Inappropriate attachments are fear-based and insecure. Inappropriate attachments make for relationships in which we are needy, overly sensitive, and constantly anxious about being rejected or abandoned. Individuals can also become emotionally distant and reject intimacy to protect themselves from hurt. Communication becomes unpredictable, depending upon the mood, or can also become completely nonexistent to avoid conflict.

Inappropriate attachments can cause individuals to act like emotional "predators" or "prey." Predators participate in relationships solely to feed their own emotional needs. To one extreme, a predatory individual will abuse or bully others to gain a sense of power and numb their insecurities. The opposite is someone that can't help but rescue others for a sense of significance. This behavior, also known as "knight-in-shining-armor syndrome," may not seem predatory at first, but the emotional hunger is what reveals its true nature.

When we let others break our boundaries to feed their emotional hunger, we risk becoming emotional prey. We can even become emotional victims when we let others manipulate us and don't defend our boundaries.

Unfortunately, many of us become emotional predators and prey without being aware of it. The best way to determine whether we've become an emotional predator or prey is to test for the emotion of peace. Peace is the cozy feeling that everything is right in the world. When we have appropriate attachments, there will always be an authentic joy. And authentic joy always creates a feeling of peace.

Without peace, there's always a nagging feeling that something's not right. When interacting with an emotional predator, people describe it as "creepy" and "janky," or other words to describe feeling unsettled. And when acting as an emotional predator, there's always a lack of satisfaction in the relationship. There's an unsettling craving for something more from the other person, instead of feeling peace in the knowledge that being in the relationship itself is enough. These sensations may be subtle, but they're always worth investigating.

Attachment Pain and Addiction

When individuals can't develop appropriate attachments, they can experience insecure attachment pains such as rejection and fear of abandonment. To self-medicate this pain, they'll try to satisfy their cravings for joy through various substitutes such as certain behaviors, experiences, events, substances, and, as mentioned, inappropriate attachments to other people.

An example is emotional eating. When we grow up, we're meant to bond with people through sharing meals. As the expression goes, it's hard to remain enemies when people have "break bread" together. But when we can't develop appropriate attachments with those sharing the food, we'll attach to the food itself. The result is emotional eating. We eat to fill a craving that should be satisfied with authentic joy. We become just like predators that hunt for their next meal. And while bingeing on our cravings may be enjoyable at the moment, we don't have any peace because it's not emotionally satisfying and will never be. Instead, we feel shame that causes more pain.

The cycle of pain, bingeing, shame, and more pain is common to all patterns of addiction. Those addicted to drugs, sex, video games, and even exercise share the same experience. But the opposite of having an addiction is a sense of connection. When we learn to develop appropriate attachments, we strengthen our connections with others through bonds of joy, breaking the power of addiction. And by strengthening our brain's joy center, full recovery from the addiction is possible.

Training the Brain for Appropriate Attachment

The attachment center of our brains lights up when we feel like being with someone because of joy. These are the people we're glad to be with, in strength but especially in weakness. They're the first individuals we want to share our victories with, like good news or an achievement. They're also the people we seek to feel safe with when experiencing discouragement and failure. Most importantly, these individuals allow us to be vulnerable despite our shame. They don't try to "fix" us. They're just glad to be with us.

Our brains are wired, at the deepest level, for joyful connection. As demonstrated, our attachment center is based completely upon relationships. We experience the greatest pleasures from joyful attachment. We also feel tremendous pain from any relational loss.

Training the brain for appropriate attachment commences with the first relay runner on Team Qortex. We start the race with the joy baton. We coach each runner through all four stages of the Qortex Circuit to hand off the joy baton between them. And it all starts with the people that represent joy in your life.

Brain Training Exercise

In your journal, list all the people that you're glad to be with, in strength and in weakness. Again, these are individuals that you can be vulnerable with and who don't try to "fix" you. Write down the reasons they give you joy.

When complete, look at your list. What does it tell you about your attachment patterns?

Common answers to this exercise include "my kids" and "my dog" (cats too). And no doubt, children and pets can be sources of tremendous joy. But if there aren't adults on your list, especially the ones that should be closest to you, such as your spouse, this should be a concern. It may be a sign of insecure attachment patterns that are anxious or avoid emotional intimacy.

If this is you, don't worry. The rest of this book will help. Keep going.

Qortex Coaching Application

Corrective Complex is a behavior that instantly kills joy and cripples Team Qortex. To develop appropriate attachments and effectively coach others, you will need to eliminate Corrective Complex. The next chapter will teach you how.

#EQ2iQ: Tough Love for Parents

I'm going to fire a warning shot for parents. The next chapter, in many ways, has been written for parents that are trying to "fix" their children. Nothing creates more insecurity in parents than the performance and success of their children. And one of the things I enjoy least about coaching parents is telling them that "fixing" their children first starts with a brutally honest look at themselves. If you're a parent, get ready for some potential tough love.

@EDKANG99

08
CORRECTIVE COMPLEX

Corrective Complex is the knee-jerk reaction to give unsolicited advice to fix, heal, convert, teach, and direct. We all have a Corrective Complex whether we admit it or not.

Corrective Complex derives from what psychologists know as the Righting Reflex. The Righting Reflex is a natural human tendency to want to set things right for others. Although similar, there's a fine line that separates them. The difference is the Righting Reflex is about *others,* and Corrective Complex is all about *us*.

The Righting Reflex is activated when we hear *others* talking about how *their* current reality is different from how *they* want things to be. It's about *them*. Corrective Complex is different, in that it occurs when *we* want to impose how *we* want things to be. In other words, the Corrective Complex is how we project our own needs, desires, insecurities, expectations, and assumptions onto others. You could say Corrective Complex is the reason we have a Righting Reflex in the first place.

To help you picture this, think about how many people you know who always tell others what they should do before even being asked. Who in your life is always trying to fix, heal, convert, teach, or direct?

For many, it's parents or in-laws that represent the most Corrective Complex in their lives. Or it's that one friend who's always doling out advice, trying to be "helpful." Leaders can be just as guilty.

Individuals with Corrective Complex tend to remind everyone else of their past mistakes. Sometimes this is done subtly, or by throwing an entire record of transgressions right in a person's face. They also tend to focus solely on the problems, solutions, and tasks-at-hand versus trusting and prioritizing relationships. They make others tired of "walking on eggshells." So to avoid these types of people, they're not invited or included in anything if possible.

Corrective Complex can occur when we affect others with our "emotional leakage." When dealing with unresolved emotions, we can place inappropriate expectations on others to make us feel better or take responsibility for our problems. For instance, if someone's feeling insecure, they may start to get angry because they're not acknowledged. This reaction is an attempt to "correct" others.

Here are some other examples you may recognize:

- The husband telling his spouse how to *fix* a problem without taking the time to listen and empathize.
- The friend that always tries to *heal* others through a combination of pseudo counseling and pointing out the bright side by saying "at least . . ." a lot.
- The entrepreneur that's trying to *convert* everybody they meet by always selling something.
- The parent that turns every situation into a *teaching* moment, pointing out faults, even when kids are just acting like kids.
- The manager that's always *directing* by playing the "authority card" or through micromanagement.

Narcissism

Narcissists are in a constant state of Corrective Complex. At the root of narcissistic patterns is deep insecurity and inability or refusal to feel shame. They either play as the biggest victims in the room, or have egos so big it's a wonder they fit into the room in the first place.

Narcissists are always correcting others and will break any boundary to do so. They achieve this through multiple tactics. They can be passive-aggressive, constantly blaming or weaponizing shame. Another method is "gaslighting," where the narcissist will emotionally manipulate others to question their version of events and observations (if you ever feel compelled to record a conversation with a narcissist to keep facts straight, it's a sign of gaslighting). Corrective Complex from a narcissist is incredibly toxic and is emotional abuse.

The best way to neutralize the narcissist is to develop joy and appropriate boundaries. If we can be courageous and vulnerable with our strengths and weaknesses, especially when we feel shame, we become impervious to the tactics of Corrective Complex employed by the narcissist. And because of joy bonds and secure attachments, we can maintain boundaries. Narcissists always need others to fix, heal, convert, teach, and direct. Take away their power and hold your ground no matter how much the narcissist protests or tries to manipulate.

From a "Good" Place

Corrective Complex is the single biggest joy-killer in any relationship. Yet narcissism aside, Corrective Complex, for the most part, starts from a place of good intentions. As they say, however, the road to hell is often paved with good intentions. And "hell" happens to be an adequate term to describe what it feels like when bombarded with Corrective Complex.

Let me emphasize: *When you're in Corrective Complex, you've got a complex, you give others a complex, and you make the situation far more complex than it ever needs to be.*

I'm not discounting the fact you may have legitimate expertise to fix, heal, convert, teach, and direct. But remember, Corrective Complex occurs when correction is *unsolicited*. Think about how you instinctively react when someone gives you unsolicited advice, especially when you're not in the mood. We shut down, get defensive, or rebel, doing the exact opposite of the intended advice (my natural reaction is to think, *I'll show you!*).

Parents can be particularly brutal with Corrective Complex, especially adults that have achieved certain levels of success in their own lives. Parents create an "emotional legacy" for their children, which is a narrative checklist to be achieved by the child as evidence they're "good" parents. To most parents, raising the best children is a chance to prove they "got it right." But when children don't meet these expectations, parents morph into Corrective Complexers—with the best intentions of course—such as Hockey Dads, Tiger Moms, Helicopter Parents, and the latest incarnation, "Snowplow Parents."

Finally, one of the most heinous forms of Corrective Complex happens during grief. Imagine someone who just lost a family member to terminal illness. At that point, nothing anybody says can make things better. Yet out of sympathy, people will resort to Corrective Complex with statements such as, "They're in a better place," or, "There's a reason for everything." Even saying, "Everything's going to be OK," is a form of Corrective Complex, and inappropriate at that moment.

Collaborative Change

The opposite of the Corrective Complex is Collaborative Change. Collaborative Change starts with humbling yourself and respecting that—although you may know what to do and genuinely want the best for others—*they* are the experts in what *they* need for *their* change.

And when they're ready, they'll invite you to collaborate with them on the possibility of such change. Collaborative Change, therefore, happens best when everybody feels joy with each other.

Collaborative Change is the foundation for all Qortex Coaching. To learn Collaborative Change, first eliminate the Corrective Complex. Corrective Complex is the number one public enemy of joy. I can't reinforce this enough. Corrective Complex *murders* joy.

Brain Training Exercise

Start eliminating Corrective Complex—completely. Aggressively strip your system of any hint of it. Doing this is easier if you develop the self-awareness to recognize Corrective Complex in the first place.

Start paying attention to instances of Corrective Complex throughout the day. Notice when others give you unsolicited advice trying to fix, heal, convert, teach, or direct you. Make mental notes when you do the same to others. Reflect on how Corrective Complex made you feel and how it might have made others feel the same.

W.A.I.T before Corrective Complex

Try the W.A.I.T. technique. W.A.I.T. is an acronym for *What am I thinking?* and *Why am I talking?*

During the next conversation, W.A.I.T. before saying anything. I literally mean pause before speaking. Then ask yourself, *What am I thinking?* Then pause again before asking, *Why am I talking?* The pause your brain takes to W.A.I.T. provides enough time to organize your thoughts and engage your prefrontal cortex. It will control the urge for Corrective Complex. If you do find yourself in Corrective Complex, *say nothing*. And if you must say something, acknowledge what they tell you and thank them for sharing.

In an emotional situation with Corrective Complex, use the "Courage 3-2-1" technique. Imagine someone has just unloaded Corrective

Complex on you, causing an emotional reaction. Or you've just caught yourself on the verge of Corrective Complex because of some emotional leakage. Take a deep breath, then say, "I feel courage," count down from three, and snap your fingers. Keep taking deep breaths until you're calm.

Use your journal for reflection. Keep written accounts of experiences and how you're working towards eliminating Corrective Complex. The more you journal, the better your brain will retain this training.

Qortex Coaching Application

Identify the people in your life who operate with little-to-no Corrective Complex, and instead help you with Collaborative Change. Tell them how you appreciate what they do when you can. Call them, write a letter, or take them out for coffee. Explain to them what you're learning about Corrective Complex is and thank them for avoiding it in your relationship.

Avoid the temptation to approach people and "correct" their Corrective Complex. As you've probably figured out, if this is unsolicited, you'll be in Corrective Complex yourself. Two wrongs don't make a right, and that goes for Corrective Complex.

The best way to help others with Corrective Complex is to be vulnerable with your habits of Corrective Complex and what you're learning to do instead. Explain how you're doing everything possible to eliminate Corrective Complex and develop more joy in your life. If they start asking questions, then you're entering Collaborative Change. But if they don't want to go there, respect where they are and leave things be. Keep this in mind: It's always better to be harmless rather than helpful.

#EQ2iQ: When Children Need Correction

Parents are continually amazed by how eliminating Corrective Complex, when parenting, seems to have an immediate positive effect on their children. Without the weight of Corrective Complex, children automatically respond with joy, which provides a natural environment for healthy development. Beyond their children, parents themselves feel free of fear and expectation. So, before trying to "fix" their children, parents should take a good hard look at their Corrective Complex.

The next step is learning the fine line between Corrective Complex and the necessary corrective interventions a child needs for maturity. The younger and more immature a child is, the more unsolicited interventions they'll require. But if adults aren't careful, Corrective Complex can become normalized and create low-joy environments that suffocate their children and family dynamic. Coaching requires a balance between the current cognitive capacity of the child and the responsibility of a parent to guide them towards emotional maturity.

There's a distinct difference between a child acting out of emotional immaturity versus conscious rebellion. As an example, a child may spill a glass of milk because they're clumsy, or knock it off the table out of anger. When correcting a child for simply being a child, parents may cause their child to start to develop insecure attachment styles. At the same time, if there isn't an immediate confrontation after inappropriate behavior, children will lack self-regulation and social skills in the future. Therefore, it's not considered Corrective Complex to tell a child their behavior is inappropriate. Statements such as, "That is enough," and, "Your actions are unacceptable," are fair and appropriate.

Every child should know they're loved and accepted no matter what they're feeling. All emotions are acceptable. But they must also learn that their emotional responses can be appropriate and inappropriate. We can coach a child to understand the difference. In the heat of an emotional moment, it's acceptable to tell a child, "It's OK to feel that way, but your response is inappropriate."

Children need to understand the difference between appropriate and inappropriate shame. Appropriate shame causes the brain to say, "I want to hide because I *did* something bad," whereas inappropriate shame says, "I want to hide because I *am* bad." Appropriate shame relates to action. Inappropriate shame, which comes from a toxic form of Corrective Complex, attacks a child's identity.

To teach appropriate shame to children, start by sharing how their actions make us feel. Telling a child, "I feel angry that you're lying about your actions," creates appropriate shame in the brain, which leads to a coaching opportunity. By sharing our feelings, it demonstrates vulnerability and courage as adults. But a statement like "Stop lying" doesn't provide enough clarification from a cognitive standpoint, which can lead to toxic shame. Even worse is saying, "You're a liar," which, although it may be a technically truthful statement, can cause toxic shame and trauma.

If we don't confront children with their inappropriate behavior, we rob them of an opportunity to develop emotional intelligence, agility, responsibility, and maturity. Many parents are afraid to have this type of confrontation and resort to passive aggression. Let's go back to the glass of milk. If it was knocked over by accident, then there's no need for correction. If a child refuses to help clean up, however, and instead chooses to protest because it was just an accident, then a coaching moment has presented itself. It's fair for the parent to say, "I'm not angry that you spilled the milk. I accept you didn't do it intentionally. I feel angry because you're not willing to take responsibility and help clean it up."

Corrective Complex and discipline are not the same. Unfortunately, the term "discipline" has attained a negative connotation. Every child needs to learn discipline, which involves correction. But all discipline can be coached with joy. Every elite athlete undergoes discipline for performance, especially in team sports. In the same way, when we discipline children while maintaining joy, they develop the emotional capacity to thrive and win. But if the discipline is nothing but Corrective Complex in disguise—without joy—the opposite effect will occur.

Distracting a child from their feelings or fixing the source of an unpleasant emotion is also a form of Corrective Complex. Parents will try to shelter their children from pain using "emotional bubble wrap." The general rule for parenting is to never do something for a child they can do for themselves—this includes processing emotions.

For instance, if a child is devastated that their pet goldfish died, the following are all forms of Corrective Complex:

- "Stop crying."
- "Grow up. It was just a fish."
- "Let's go buy another one."
- "That's what happens when fish get old."
- "Ice cream will make you feel better."
- "How about a puppy?"

Sheltering children from painful emotions such as sadness and grief may seem to help in the short term, but in the long run, it will stunt their emotional maturity. The same goes for accidents. If a child inadvertently causes harm, telling them it's not their fault and ignoring the shock is Corrective Complex. Instead, coaching a child to normalize emotions and process them for an appropriate response is not Corrective Complex, but Collaborative Change.

@EDKANG99

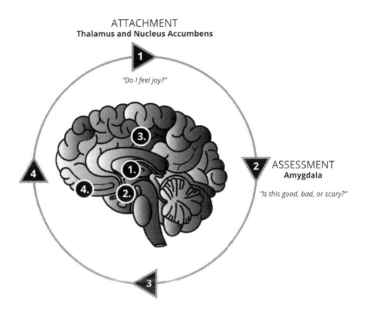

09
STAGE 2: ASSESSMENT
APPROPRIATELY ASSESSING YOURSELF AND OTHERS

The act of assessment is to evaluate or estimate the nature, quality, or ability of someone or something. Assessment is the second stage of the Qortex Circuit. In stage one, the brain processes experiences through the attachment center. Now, in stage two, our brains assess by asking, "Is this good, bad, or scary?"

It's human nature to assess the world through the lens of good, bad, and scary. Evolutionarily speaking, it's how we've learned to survive. When we bite into a freshly baked muffin, we think, *good!* Whereas a moldy piece of bread makes us think, *bad,* and causes us to throw it out. A cute puppy is *good*. A snarling dog off its leash is *bad* and *scary*. A brightly lit street is *good*. The dark alley behind the street is just *scary*.

It's also human nature to turn assessments into judgments, which happens when we "judge a book by its cover." It takes a mere fraction of a second to make an assessment that turns into a snap-judgment. And because this process happens in the emotional part of the brain, assessments occur faster than our rational brains realize.

Snap judgments can be helpful. Quarterbacks make snap judgments to pick targets and throw touchdowns. Police officers have even less time when drawing firearms in an escalating confrontation. But what happens when our emotions get in the way? Researchers have found it takes less time than the blink of an eye for someone to make a snap judgment and form an opinion about another person. The issue occurs when snap judgments overpower decision making. Even with all the information at hand, our emotional brains can hijack the process.

The Amygdala

The amygdala is an almond-shaped structure located close to the hippocampus in the frontal portion of the temporal lobe. Like most brain structures, we have two amygdalae.

As its base function, the amygdala is responsible for perceiving any fear and other emotions to prepare us for emergencies. As part of the limbic system (the emotional brain), the amygdala is considered an "emotional library" that processes memory, decision-making, and emotional responses such as anxiety and aggression.

The amygdala connects directly to our stress response systems. After emotionally processing a stressful situation, the amygdala sends a distress signal to the hypothalamus. The hypothalamus then acts as a command center, preparing the body for fight or flight by charging up our sympathetic nervous system, like pressing the gas pedal on a car. Adrenaline and cortisol are released into our systems, providing a burst of energy. Then a set of physical responses is initiated, including pumping more blood to our muscles (meaning there's less blood in the brain for thinking).

Appropriate and Inappropriate Assessment

Just like attachment, we can make appropriate and inappropriate assessments, which include assessing yourself and assessing others.

When assessments are inappropriate, such as an emotional judgment, the Qortex Circuit gets stuck. Instead of joy, fear becomes the dominant motivator. We begin to see everything as a scary problem to solve. We enter a sort of "survival mode."

If our sympathetic nervous system is like the gas, the parasympathetic nervous system is the brake. But being stuck in fear, caused by inappropriate assessments, is like constantly pressing the gas pedal while the car is parked. Our systems stay revved up, which creates chronic stress. After a while, the engine will break down. In the same way, our bodies can also break down and become susceptible to health problems. Chronic stress can lead to damaged blood vessels and arteries, increased blood pressure, and increased risk of heart attack, stroke, and disease. All of this doesn't even begin to address the effects on long-term mental health.

Another way our systems can respond from being stuck in stage two is emotional eating. Stress causes our bodies to produce extra cortisol. And elevated cortisol levels cause our bodies to attempt to replenish energy stores that deplete from a continual state of stress. Cortisol increases appetite, so we want to eat more for extra energy, which increases the storage of unused nutrients as fat. So, when someone says they "eat their stress," that's a precise way to describe what they're doing.

Training the Brain for Appropriate Assessment

With stage two Qortex coaching, we can train our brains to make appropriate assessments. Then we'll no longer make emotional judgments. Instead of constantly revving our brains with fear, we can learn to assess a situation and respond in an appropriate manner.

Making appropriate assessments involves the skill of emotional regulation. Emotional regulation is the ability to respond to a wide variety of emotions in an acceptable and productive way. Without emotional regulation, all the talent, ability, and knowledge we possess are useless. How can we trust ourselves to perform when our performance can get emotionally hijacked at any moment?

Improving our capacity for emotional regulation allows us to perform with focus, resolve conflicts, and use our entire brain capacity for creative problem-solving. People who effectively regulate their emotions are also resilient. They've learned to do hard things and bounce back quickly when there are setbacks. We trust these individuals to perform and handle themselves appropriately in every situation.

If you've been practicing the "Courage 3-2-1" technique, you're already training your brain for emotional regulation. I encourage you to continue. The technique is training you for mindfulness, which has a proven effect on stress reduction.

The next way to train your brain for appropriate assessment is to stop making emotional experiences good, bad, or scary. To do this, we're going to take the "Courage 3-2-1" technique to the next level.

First, remember the amygdala and our stress response systems are designed to protect us. They're how we respond quickly to danger—without pausing to think—like swerving to avoid an accident or defending ourselves during a physical attack. Therefore there's no intention to eliminate the stress response like Corrective Complex. What we can do is train the brain to make productive assessments and courageous choices regardless of the good, bad, or scary.

Brain Training Exercise

You're going to start training your brain to operate consistently with courage. To do this, you'll develop courageous habits and regulate fear. It will help take inappropriate assessments and reframe them into appropriate ones. You can then follow through with the appropriate action and move your Qortex Circuit to stage three.

#10MCD

#10MCD stands for a "10-minute courage drill," and it's the best way to develop any habit, by doing it ten minutes at a time. Whether it's exercise, studying for a test, or meditation, ten minutes is enough time for adequate practice but not enough time to trigger resistance in the brain. Ten minutes can create momentum quickly, versus undertaking a daunting task that may take hours. Ten minutes is also short enough to be "filler time" that's easily found throughout the day, like on the bus or during lunch. And by building momentum, ten minutes can easily expand to twenty, thirty, and sixty.

Adding the emotion of courage makes the #10MCD technique even more effective. To our brains, new information combined with the right emotion like courage creates long-term learning.

The #10MCD involves making plans for change that take ten minutes at a time. But before performing the activity, you'll say, "I feel courage, 3-2-1," and snap your fingers. Note that this will only be effective if you've extensively practiced the "Courage 3-2-1" technique, which was designed to only take ten minutes for this very reason.

It's important to avoid looking past the ten minutes and too far into the future. Be intentional and stay in the moment, at least for the first time you try it. And make sure to spend the entire ten minutes directly on the activity.

For example, if you want to start an exercise regime, don't get dressed and drive to the gym. You'll have already spent the entire ten minutes. Instead, say, "I feel courage," count down from three, snap your fingers, and immediately go for a walk. Stop after exactly ten minutes, no matter how you feel. Chances are you'll be tempted to do more.

Don't. Plan for another ten minutes the next day instead. You'll know when to increase time and intensity. But most importantly, if you start feeling resistance in your brain, fall back to ten minutes. And don't forget, always snap your fingers after saying, "I feel courage, 3-2-1!"

The #10MCD will work for pretty much everything. Try learning a new language, writing a book, or turning off all electronics to sit quietly for ten minutes. You can even start a side-hustle business in just ten minutes a day. Write a blog or record a video for social media. Make a sales call. Brainstorm and make a list in your journal of what you can accomplish in ten minutes.

With more complex projects, break them down into multiple tasks that can take ten minutes at first. Get creative. But always prioritize consistency over intensity. And again, don't forget the courage!

Regulating F.E.A.R.

When we use the word "stress," it's often code for "false expectations appearing real," or F.E.A.R. for short. F.E.A.R. occurs when we make inappropriate assessments about what's good, bad, and scary.

Take the fear of public speaking. We all have expectations in our minds of what "good" public speaking is. But we also imagine all the "bad" things that might happen. Our brains process public speaking through the assessment center. If our emotional library links public speaking to memories such as insecurity, embarrassment, or rejection, we'll start developing false expectations that appear real. F.E.A.R. triggers a stress response. And without emotional regulation, we'll get stuck in that F.E.A.R., whatever it is.

Here is a brain training exercise for F.E.A.R. regulation.

Step 1: Acknowledge the F.E.A.R with self-talk.

Acknowledging F.E.A.R. using self-talk is the first step. Self-talk is a transformation skill. Just pausing to acknowledge any good and bad expectations gives your brain a chance to pump the brakes on the stress response. It might go something like this:

> "OK, Ed, you're totally stressing out. Let's take a breath and think. Breathe man."
>
> "Alright, what am I expecting? What's the best- and worst-case scenario?"
>
> "Yeah . . . I'm afraid this is going to be a total disaster. In fact, I think it already is!"
>
> "More deep breaths, Ed, in and out. There you go. . . ."

The above might seem a touch dramatic, even comical, but it's how it sometimes goes.

Step 2: Ask, "What would courage look like right now?"

The fastest way to break through F.E.A.R. is an immediate act of courage. Trust your brain and quickly think about one action you can do right then and there. It needs to be a small enough step to be immediately actionable, yet big enough to require courage. Most likely, you'll already know what it is.

Here are some examples:

- Introducing yourself to a potential contact at a networking event.
- Emailing your manager to book an appointment.
- Sending an apology text to your spouse.
- Opening your bills and sorting which ones to pay first.
- Telling a colleague how nervous you are and asking for constructive feedback.
- Writing down a list of pros and cons to a major decision.

Step 3: Say, "I feel courage 3-2-1," snap your fingers, and do it.

After snapping your fingers, stop thinking, and start doing. Don't pause or wait to rethink.

Wayne Gretzky used to say, "You miss 100% of the shots you don't take." Michael Jordan said, "I never looked at the consequences of missing a big shot. . . . When you think about the consequences, you always think of a negative result." Jordan also said, "Live the moment for the moment."

The point is, take the first shot, whatever it is. The result isn't as important as the act of courage itself. For Team Qortex, courage is not the absence of fear, but the willingness to try despite feeling fear. This practice will train your brain to form new neural pathways for emotional regulation.

Give these steps a try. Keep a journal of every time you:

- **Step 1:** Acknowledge the F.E.A.R with self-talk.
- **Step 2:** Ask, "What would courage look like right now?"
- **Step 3:** Say, "I feel courage 3-2-1," snap your fingers, and do it.

Then reflect on the results. Did your false expectation become a reality? What did you learn each time? Make a note of any changes you observe in yourself.

Qortex Coaching Application

Have a conversation with someone and ask them what their F.E.A.R. is. Don't try to help or coach them. Just listen and ask questions as needed. That's it. You are getting your brain ready for empathy, which will serve you in the next stage of the Qortex Circuit. But first, start practicing how to listen without Corrective Complex.

#EQ2iQ: Fear, Terror, Anger, and Rage

At 15 months, a switch flips in the assessment center of a child's brain that activates the capacity for terror and rage in the limbic system. Terror occurs when fear becomes mixed with hopeless despair. The same happens with rage. When anger mixes with hopeless despair, a child feels enraged (inward rage). In hopeless despair, the brain thinks, *I've tried everything and can't do anything else.* Therefore, learning to regulate hopeless despair will disconnect the source of power for terror and rage.

Telling a child in hopeless despair what to do, or how to fix their problems, is Corrective Complex. The child won't learn to regulate the emotion but will constantly expect rescue. Instead, coach the child with empathy and ask open questions about how to possibly address hopeless despair.

Here are some steps to try:

- **Step 1:** Acknowledge the fear or anger: "That must make you scared/angry."
- **Step 2:** Empathize: "I understand how you feel. I get scared/angry too."
- **Step 3:** Ask what they want to do: "What do you want to do?"
- **Step 4:** Explore other options: "What else could you do?"
- **Step 5:** Provide suggestions as necessary: "How about trying this?"
- **Step 6:** Let them make a final decision and support them: "Let's give that a try and see what happens."
- **Step 7:** Address failure with joy: "If it doesn't work we can try something else. I'm just glad we're figuring it out together."

10
METACOGNITIVE REFLECTION

Metacognitive reflection is an incredibly useful skill to develop emotional intelligence, agility, responsibility, and maturity. Unfortunately, it's also one of the most overlooked skills taught today.

Metacognitive reflection is different than self-reflection. Self-reflection focuses on assessing and analyzing one's performance. Metacognitive reflection is the next level because it involves "thinking about thinking" for self-improvement. And with the inclusion of emotions in this process, we automatically develop EQ.

Practicing metacognitive reflection will boost every stage of the Qortex Circuit. The process of metacognitive reflection involves pondering the *what*, *when*, *how*, and *who* through a series of EQ-based internal questions.

1. **What:** *What am I feeling? What am I observing? What am I thinking?*
2. **When:** *When do I feel this? When do I respond? When should I respond?*
3. **How:** *How did I get here? How can I take responsibility?*
4. **Who:** *Who am I? Who do I want to be? Whom do I want to be me with?*

Starts with an Emotional Vocabulary

To be effective at the skill of metacognitive reflection, we must learn how to identify emotions accurately and quickly. According to Dr. Travis Bradberry, author of *Emotional Intelligence 2.0*, although we all experience emotions, only 36% of people can accurately identify emotions in real time as they occur. When emotions go unlabelled, they can be misunderstood and lead to inappropriate choices and actions. Thus, an expanded emotional vocabulary is highly helpful.

For example, many people default to describing their emotional state as feeling "bad" or "stressed." But with a robust emotional vocabulary, you can be more accurate and use words like "disappointed," "resentful," or "intimidated." Although these emotions can be generalized under terms like "bad" or "stress," they're each quite different in their respective connotations. And the more accurate you are, the better you can understand the causes and resolve them with the appropriate course of action.

After you've determined what emotions you're feeling (*what*), you can begin to identify patterns associated with those emotions (*when*). Then you can reflect on how you came to develop those patterns. The source and patterns reveal where you can, and should, take responsibility (*how*). Finally, you can use all this data to reflect and activate your identity (*who*).

Team Qortex

By the time you've finished any act of metacognitive reflection, you will have stimulated every brain center of the Qortex Circuit. It's like giving each runner on Team Qortex a healthy workout and coaching.

Metacognitive reflection will prepare your brain for self-regulation. You won't be reactionary with your emotions. Instead, you'll have already reflected on them, which develops the neural pathways to quickly and accurately identify emotions and resulting patterns, and finally be prepared to act with responsibility.

Brain Training Exercise

Start working on your metacognitive reflection skills. In your journal, write down what you're feeling at this very moment. Write down as many emotions that come to mind. But avoid words like "good," "fine," or "normal."

Try looking up synonyms to common emotions you already know. Use www.thesaurus.com and start expanding your emotional vocabulary. You'll be improving your emotional intelligence at the same time. Also, start paying attention to different emotions people use, especially any that particularly strike you. Make a mental note. Even better, text it to yourself or jot it in a notebook. It all helps.

Qortex Coaching Application

Start asking others how they feel right at that moment. Pay attention to how they respond. Make a note of how many people can accurately identify their emotions beyond the typical cliché responses.

One thing you'll start to notice is how often we confuse what we feel with what we think. For example, someone might say, "I feel like you're not listening to me," which is what that person thinks, not what they feel. Although this practice is commonly accepted, it prevents us from developing emotional intelligence and agility.

Individuals with high EQ can articulate the difference between what they feel—with robust emotional vocabulary—and what they think. Instead of "I feel like you're not listening to me," how much more effective would it be if someone said, "I'm starting to feel a little insecure because I think you're not listening to me," See how much difference emotional intelligence makes?

#EQ2iQ: Teach Children Emotional Vocabulary

It's never too early to teach children emotional vocabulary. By the time they've reached three years of age, children should be able to make "I feel" statements with emotions. They may not know exactly every nuance of what particular emotions mean, but sharing how they feel should be normalized behavior. Normalizing emotional statements is as important as teaching the alphabet and counting numbers. Learning emotions should be encouraged and celebrated the same way as any other academic achievement.

As children age, you can introduce them to more complex emotional vocabulary and ask them to repeat it. Repetition will improve metacognition and applies to both pleasant and unpleasant emotions. For example, you can say, "What you're describing is feeling anticipation, which means you're thinking about what might happen next. Try saying, 'I feel anticipation.'"

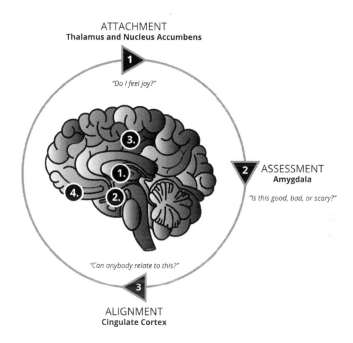

11
STAGE 3: ALIGNMENT
APPROPRIATELY ALIGNING YOURSELF AND OTHERS

Every vehicle requires maintenance of its wheel alignment. A vehicle is easier to handle while driving when the wheels are properly aligned. When wheels are out of alignment, there's a risk of tire damage and accidents, because the vehicle becomes harder to control.

Just like any vehicle, we also need to maintain emotional alignment. But instead of wheels, we align ourselves to relationships. It all starts by aligning what we feel with what we think and what we do. We then align ourselves with other people, and they align with us. The more alignment there is, the more our worlds are synchronized and the more synergy we have with the people in our lives. And when people operate synergistically, anything is possible.

At stage three of the Qortex Circuit, the brain asks, "Can anybody relate to this?" Our brain compares responses we observe from other people and how they appear to be relating to our own experience. We want to know if others perceive reality the way we do.

Cingulate Cortex

The cingulate cortex is the alignment center of the brain. Just like the amygdala, it is considered part of the limbic system. It contributes to emotion formation and processing, learning, and memory. Receiving input from the thalamus and neocortex, it plays a major role in linking motivational outcomes to behavior. For instance, when we experience a positive emotional response from a particular action, the cingulate cortex helps us learn from it. It's the layer of the brain that helps align information and emotion for long-term learning.

When two people are aligned, their brains can achieve something called a "mutual mind state." Mutual mind state occurs during face-to-face interactions and is powerful. If one person has a more organized and trained brain, the other person's brain will start to self-organize and train itself just by the interaction. This neuroscientific evidence proves something we've always been told: You are indeed the average of the ten people you hang out with the most.

Appropriate and Inappropriate Alignment

Appropriate alignments involve synchronization and synergy. When we're appropriately aligned, we feel connected to other people and have a social awareness of what's happening in our relationships. And when aligned with joy, we never feel isolated. We also work more effectively with others.

With inappropriate alignments, people act socially awkward and misread relationships. We start to see or invent issues in relationships or social situations that are not the reality. We misread people and are unable to empathize. Instead, our relationships become self-serving and transactional. They lack emotional reciprocity, which is a core psychological need we all have.

People align their relationships based on different types of bonds. There are two-way, three-way, and four-way bonds. These bonds can be appropriate or inappropriate.

Two-way bonds occur, as implied, between two people. When the bond is appropriate, it represents the highest potential for emotional intimacy, such as between a married couple. Two-way bonds, however, can become inappropriate when there are different power dynamics with discrepancies between levels of emotional maturity. These relationships can become co-dependent based on fear, or emotionally abusive. Therefore, two-way bonds are the most appropriate between committed couples.

Three-way bonds, when appropriate, are the healthiest. They maximize joy potential while avoiding the traps of two-way bonds. Adding a third bond creates balance, integrity, and accountability. Like a tripod, the relationship is more stable. Different levels of emotional maturity can exist without creating a dangerous relationship. Our brains are designed to receive and respond best within three-way bonds. They emulate the secure attachment in a relationship between a child and two parents.

It's important to understand that a two-way-bond-plus-one should not be mistaken for a three-way bond. Another way to describe this is when someone becomes a "third wheel" to a two-way bond. For example, a married couple that tries to add a third romantic partner can create competitive dynamics that divide rather than strengthen them. Another example is when a child takes the side of one parent and the two gang up on the other one. As soon as power dynamics or "social politics" enter the picture, three-way bonds can splinter.

Four-way bonds optimize functional relationships where one member is the leader, such as at work. In this configuration, the leader receives the support of the three-way bond between other members. And the three can support each other as they support the leader. To be appropriate, the group must have a relatively flat power structure with a sense of psychological safety. The leader should be the "first among equals" and should be authoritative without being authoritarian. However, without transparency and integrity, four-way bonds become inappropriate and easily fragile.

The bonds I describe here are to maximize joy and practice emotional intelligence, agility, responsibility, and maturity. They also apply to any coaching arrangement. Obviously, we can bond to more than two or three people. We can bond with many others through common identities such as an organization, ethnicity, or culture. We can also form bonds with multitudes through experiences, such as cheering for our favorite sports team or participating in a national celebration. But most of the time, large group bonds are made up of networks of two-, three-, and four-way bonds.

Training the Brain for Appropriate Alignment

The fastest way to train the brain for appropriate alignments is by learning empathy. At its most basic level, empathy is the ability to understand and share the feelings of others. But empathy, from a brain training perspective, goes much deeper.

There are four levels of empathy we can learn:

1. **Cognitive Empathy:** "I think I know how you feel."
2. **Emotional Empathy:** "I feel how you feel."
3. **Compassionate Empathy:** "I'm moved by how you feel."
4. **Appreciative Empathy:** "I appreciate how you feel."

Empathy allows us to align with others appropriately. Empathy also helps us know when and what to change if alignments become inappropriate. It also helps others be vulnerable with us, which creates deeper joy bonds. Empathy is how people are drawn to self-organize, synchronize, and synergize with each other.

Trust

The neurochemical oxytocin can help accelerate empathy. When we experience trust from others, even strangers, our brains produce oxytocin. Our bodies release oxytocin when we snuggle or bond socially, which is how it got nicknamed the "love" or "cuddle" hormone. Oxytocin increases our ability to understand other people's emotions and is known to help teams form faster by inducing members to work harder together and sacrifice for each other.

Brain Training Exercise

There are six steps to training your brain for four levels of empathy and trust. These steps prepare your brain for the next stage of the Qortex Circuit. You'll also notice they build upon the "Courage 3-2-1" technique.

Step 1: List the important people in your life.

In a journal, draw a circle with your name in the center. Then start creating a map of connections, starting with those that are closest to you, such as your spouse. The more connected and important they are, the closer to your circle they should be.

Step 2: "What do I think they're feeling?" (Cognitive Empathy)

Pick a name and start to brainstorm what you think they're feeling. This exercise is the start of cognitive empathy. On a new page, if needed, write whatever comes to mind. But make sure you write what you think they feel instead of what you think they *think*, by using emotional vocabulary. As you've learned, when most people use the word "feel" they mean "think." The two get confused. So instead of, "They feel like there isn't enough time in the day," it should be, "They feel anxious and overwhelmed because there isn't enough time in the day."

Step 3: "When do I feel the same feeling?" (Emotional Empathy)

Next, write down the times you might feel the same thing. Here, you're training your brain for emotional empathy. And this doesn't have to be a similar situation. Use your imagination. You can relate it to different experiences in your life—past or current and ongoing. For example, if the person is feeling sad about the loss of a promotion, you may write, "I felt the same way when I wasn't picked as captain of my hockey team last year," or, "I feel the same way every year when my team announces the captains."

Step 4: "How could I respond to how they are feeling?" (Compassionate Empathy)

Now it's time for compassionate empathy. This level of empathy moves us to appropriate action. Make a list of how you could respond to what they're feeling. It may be as simple as sending them an email acknowledging an achievement, or taking responsibility for your contribution to some conflict. What's most important is that your response is compassionate and appropriate.

A note of caution. Compassion can sometimes be confused with sympathy. Sympathy is feeling sorry and can become overwhelming, leading to patterns of rescuing or enabling. The result will always be an inappropriate alignment. Writing in a journal gives you time to evaluate the difference.

You don't have to act on your response plan. It's is not a to-do list of obligations. Don't feel pressure, but do consider what courage would look like if you were to act. You'll know when and how to act better than anybody else. Trust yourself and take courage.

Step 5: "Who do I appreciate them being to me?" (Appreciative Empathy)

Next, write down everything you appreciate about their identities. Appreciate who they are to you, as well as what they do. For example, instead of, "I appreciate the pies my mother bakes," try writing, "A mother that always took the time to learn the best recipes for our family and me."

Here is a tip: Refer to this list when you find yourself "relationally offline" with these individuals. Your brain will start to align itself and reactivate your Qortex Circuit back to stage three.

Step 6: Plan a courageous demonstration of trust.

We're now going to infuse the relationship with oxytocin, increasing trust and empathy. Here are some ideas to get you started, but try being creative.

- Ask their opinion on something important. Ask what they'd do. Earnestly consider their input.
- Confide in them and be transparent. Share an insecurity or aspiration. Thank them for being trustworthy.
- Ask them to plan something. Start small. Be open. Give constructive feedback when appropriate.
- Plan a project together that takes equal responsibility. Be clear on roles and responsibilities.
- Take their side. Let them win an argument and make the final decision.
- Give them veto power over a decision you've made. Let them use it any time.

Remember, this demonstration will require courage. There can be no trust without courage.

Qortex Coaching Application

Follow the six steps and then put your courageous demonstration of trust into action. Journal any reflections on how things go.

From this point on, practice the different levels of empathy whenever interacting with others. Go through this checklist:

1. "I think you feel . . ." (Cognitive Empathy)
2. "I feel you feel . . ." (Emotional Empathy)
3. "I'm moved to . . ." (Compassionate Empathy)
4. "I appreciate . . ." (Appreciative Empathy)

Tell people what your empathy tells you. Test yourself. You can even try one type of empathy per day.

The more you practice each level, the more automatic these skills will become. And the more trust you'll build, creating appropriate alignments.

#EQ2iQ: Three Things Every Child Needs to Hear for Alignment

"I love you."

"I'm sorry."

"I believe in you."

When you develop empathy, you'll know when to say each. Say these sincerely and often to a child, then watch them transform. Try it and see what happens.

12
COLLABORATIVE CHANGE TALKS

To review, Corrective Complex occurs when we give unsolicited advice to fix, heal, convert, teach, and direct. By now, you should be very aware of Corrective Complex around you and within you. Hopefully, you're starting to see the benefits of eliminating it from your life.

As also introduced, the opposite of Corrective Complex is Collaborative Change. Collaborative Change is just as the name implies. It's a collaborative conversation that leads to change while respecting every individual's identity and autonomy.

The natural question is, "How can we most effectively move from Corrective Complex to Collaborative Change?" After all, there must be a time and place for fixing, healing, converting, teaching, and directing, right? Because of this, another common question is, "Can Corrective Complex ever be a good thing?"

The answer is no. Although Corrective Complex may at times get results, they're short term at best. Without joy, there's no sustainable trust and engagement. And more importantly, emotional maturity can't be achieved.

Think of Corrective Complex and Collaborative Change as two opposite sides of a chasm. To cross the gap, we build a bridge. A bridge that's built with EQ using metacognitive reflection.

The EQ Bridge

In chapter nine, you learned a model for metacognitive reflection. It involved asking four questions based on the four cornerstones of EQ.

1. **What:** Emotional Intelligence
2. **When:** Emotional Agility
3. **How:** Emotional Responsibility
4. **Who:** Emotional Maturity

The same model can be used to initiate Collaborative Change. Using this metacognitive technique during a conversation helps develop empathy and also trains the other person's brain. You achieve this by activating the brain's mirror neurons. Mirror neurons help us imitate observed behaviors and learn. But they also provide the capacity to feel what others feel, empathize, and understand those feelings. In other words, mirror neurons act as the bridge between people's brains which helps us cross the gap to Collaborative Change.

The following are four scenarios where our EQ-based metacognitive model can be used to initiate Collaborative Change. But first, it's important to understand this model works best after you've done metacognitive reflection for yourself. Always be asking yourself:

1. **What:** *What am I feeling? What am I observing? What am I thinking?*
2. **When:** *When do I feel this? When do I respond? When should I respond?*
3. **How:** *How did I get here? How can I take responsibility?*
4. **Who:** *Who am I? Who do I want to be? Whom do I want to be me with?*

Next, each of these conversations should start with consent. Typically, you'll start by establishing your intentions and asking permission to have a conversation in the first place. These models don't work if they're spontaneous or thrown out in the heat of an emotional moment. It also helps if you politely ask for time to speak without interruption. Assure them they'll have an opportunity to provide feedback.

Scenario 1: Emotional Needs Talk

1. **What I feel and think**
2. **When I feel and think it**
3. **How I need help**
4. **Who I want to be and don't want to be**

It takes courage to be vulnerable and share our emotional needs. It takes even more courage and trust to ask for our emotional needs to be met. Although it's inappropriate to expect that others will always meet your emotional needs, the act of sharing and asking for help can lead to positive Collaborative Change opportunities.

Start with what you feel and think. Feelings should come first to make an emotional connection. The order also helps with emotional regulation. Then share what you're thinking. If they get defensive, explain that you only want to take responsibility for your feelings and thoughts.

> "I'm feeling insecure these days because I'm starting to think you don't enjoy spending time with me like we used to."

Share when you have similar feelings and thoughts. Share any patterns you observe without presenting a list like you're reading from a record in a file. Be specific, which will create context, grounding the conversation with facts and information. Assure them all participants in the conversation will have time to respond after your part.

> "This has been going on for the past three weekends when we just stayed at home. I experience the same when I come home and you don't greet me. Instead, you're tied up with other things like talking on the phone or the kids."

Share how you need help with a single request. Multiple requests can be overwhelming and create Corrective Complex. Be direct but not directive. Explain the emotional need behind it. Remember, this entire conversation is about you—not them. Don't blame them and demand help. If they object, explain that you don't expect them to solve the problem for you but want to be open and vulnerable with your needs.

> "I need some help here. I want to figure out a way to have time together, once a week, where it's just us. No distractions. I'd feel connected and appreciated. We'd also have fun, which I need these days."

Tell them who you want to be from having this talk. Include who you want to be to them, if pertinent. Also, share who you don't want to be. Here, you're painting a picture of the positive outcome while contrasting a negative to motivate Collaborative Change.

> "I want to be a great partner and parent to you and the kids. I don't want to be someone that takes their family for granted and makes everything about the business."

End this part of the conversation by asking an open question—a question that can't have a yes or no answer—inviting them to Collaborative Change. Typically, this is as simple as asking, "What do you think?"

Scenario 2: Conflict Talk

1. **What I'm experiencing**
2. **When I experience it**
3. **How it makes me feel conflicted**
4. **Who you are to me**

We all experience conflict at different times for a multitude of reasons. Some are more comfortable with conflict than others. Conflict based on Corrective Complex never ends well. It usually ends with an emotional winner and loser. But using EQ, it's possible to present conflict in a way that creates Collaborative Change.

Start with what you're experiencing. Present it as a series of observations rather than grievances. Make this about your experience rather than what they're doing to cause it. Also, focus on one issue. If you want to address multiple issues, plan for multiple conversations.

> "I've noticed that you don't seem very happy with my performance lately. You were very short with me at our last meeting in front of the team. And you appear to be angry when we talk."

Provide context for when the experiences have occurred. Be specific with an example or pattern. Make it factual. Don't invoke an "invisible army" by involving others to support your perspective. If they want to argue, ask politely for permission to share your side first. Assure them they'll have time to disagree or clarify their positions.

> "Specifically, I began experiencing this when we launched the new project a couple of weeks back. And when I presented my report yesterday, you didn't give

me a chance to explain my argument."

Share your conflicted feelings. Do this by presenting both sides and contrasting the problem with an opportunity (in that order). It's an approach that demonstrates a balanced perspective, looking at all sides while directly resolving the conflict. Don't make any accusations. Be vulnerable with your feelings.

> "I'm feeling conflicted here. Part of me is getting upset, and it's preventing me from staying focused. But I also know you're under a lot of pressure because the project means a lot for this company."

Assure who they are to you. Share what resolving the conflict would mean for how you see the relationship and how it would benefit.

> "You're a manager here for a reason. I'm confident this is a process issue. Figuring things out will not only help you and me but the rest of the team as well. Your leadership plays a key role for me at this company."

End this part of the conversation by asking an open question—a question that can't have a yes or no answer—inviting them to Collaborative Change. Typically, this is as simple as asking, "What do you think?"

Scenario 3: Feedback Talk

1. **What I observe**
2. **When I observe it**
3. **How I think there could be change**
4. **Who you could be**

Feedback is incredibly valuable if delivered and received correctly. The potential issue with feedback is that it can quickly turn into Corrective Complex. But when delivered with emotional intelligence, feedback can not only be constructive but also welcomed with joy.

Start with your observations. Keep them neutral from the perspective of a third-party observer. If it's personal feedback, don't make it about their character. Instead, focus on their behaviors. Also, make them your observations alone and not what you think others think (the invisible army).

> "I've observed that your grades seem to be slipping lately. You've been playing a lot more video games and messaging your friends on the phone."

Share when the observations have occurred. Be specific with details and patterns to establish context for your feedback. Carefully observe their reactions, verbally and through body language, to maintain empathy and gauge the progress of the conversation. If they object, assure them that these are only your observations, and they'll have time to respond.

> "This seems to be happening when you're supposed to be doing homework. Or right before a test."

Offer how you think one thing could change. Don't give a whole list. Start with one thing that you believe is a priority or would make the biggest difference. If you've established Collaborative Change, the more likely it is you'll be asked for more feedback when the time is appropriate.

> "I think a schedule will help you balance your leisure time and homework."

Tell them who they are and who they could be. Start with who they are to you. Then paint a picture of who they are now and who they could become if they make changes. Doing this creates what's called a "generative image," which is highly motivating from a psychological perspective. Just remember though, what you present must line up with their values. If It doesn't, they'll resist change and enter Corrective Complex.

"I care about you, and your future is important to me. I know you want to succeed too. If you find the right balance now, you'll get that job you've always dreamed of for sure."

End this part of the conversation by asking an open question—a question that can't have a yes or no answer—inviting them to Collaborative Change. Typically, this is as simple as asking, "What do you think?"

Scenario 4: Metacognitive Inquiry

1. **What are you feeling and thinking?**
2. **When does this happen?**
3. **How do you think it got this point?**
4. **Who do you want to be?**

There are times when asking the right series of questions is what's needed to bridge a conversation towards Collaborative Change. Using metacognitive inquiry can help someone "think about what they're thinking" and get them unstuck. This model is particularly effective at the beginning of any Qortex Coaching conversation.

When using this format, provide a safe and ample space for them to explore their thoughts. Affirm their processing and ask clarifying questions. Avoid making suggestions or giving advice until finished with all the questions. If they ask your opinion, let them know you'd like to ask all your questions first. Covering the entire process will provide the best information and personal connection to determine where the conversation could go next.

Don't be afraid to guide the conversation, such as pointing out the difference between thoughts and feelings. Emotions must be acknowledged to keep everybody relationally online. It also establishes empathy and makes for a more emotionally intelligent conversation. You may consider saying something to the effect of:

> "I hear what you're saying. And it makes sense. I'm wondering how you feel about it, which is different than what you think. Again, how do you feel?"

At the end of the inquiry, ask an open question to invite Collaborative Change. Asking a closed question with a "yes" or "no" answer can potentially snap the conversation into Corrective Complex. Open questions are especially important if there isn't yet an established relationship between the two of you.

Here are some examples:

- "Where do you see this going next?"
- "What would you like to do now?"
- "How can I help?"
- "Would you like me to listen more, or would you like my advice?"

Meta-Conversations

An effective technique in Qortex Coaching is starting things off with a meta-conversation. Going meta means "having a conversation about the conversation." The goal is to establish intentions and clarify the context. Meta-conversations are highly collaborative because it solicits input but also starts with consent.

Here are some examples:

> "I'd like to take a moment and establish the reason we're here. We all agree there's a problem, and that feedback would be helpful. Does anybody else have additional thoughts before we begin?"

> "I spent some time organizing my thoughts. I'd appreciate the opportunity to share them and invite us to have a candid conversation. How does that sound?"

> "Our last few conversations haven't been very productive. I think you'd agree. I want to try a different format and see if it works better. What do you think?"
>
> "Let's talk about the format for this conversation. I want to ask you some questions first to gain an understanding. Unless you have some other ideas, we can talk now or later."

Aside from being up-front, a meta-conversation can also be used to check in on how Collaborative Change is going. This an opportune time to share any observations about the conversation itself. Feedback can be solicited and then implemented quickly.

> "Can we step back for a moment and check in? How's this conversation going for you?"
>
> "You don't seem like you want to be having this talk. What should we do?"
>
> "I don't feel heard here and think I need to change my approach. How can I explain it better for you?"
>
> "Let's pause for a moment. Would it be better if we took a pause?"

Signs of Collaborative Change

The two signs that indicate Collaborative Change are courage and energy.

First, when people have entered Collaborative Change, they'll begin to speak about potential steps for courage. These will be statements that indicate the possibility of change. Second, the level of increased energy in their statements will tell you how much Collaborative Change is taking place.

For example, "I guess I could try something new," is a courageous statement but with low energy. In contrast, "I need to try something new, for sure," is courage with high energy.

When it comes to questions, the same principle applies. "What should I do again?" is different than, "What are those five steps again?" The second question is more detailed which demonstrates higher energy.

Lastly, evaluate any admissions or agreements the same way. "You're probably right," may indicate agreement but could be done begrudgingly, and the true message could be up for interpretation. But saying, "I didn't consider that. I see your point now," is an indication that metacognitive reflection has occurred.

To test for courage and energy, ask plenty of open questions such as, "What would that look like for you?" or, "How would you approach this?" Avoid making your questions too suggestive with recommendations until they are ready.

Brain Training Exercise

The best way to train your brain for Collaborative Change talks is emotional visualization. Basketball players use similar visualization exercises to practice free throws mentally. For Collaborative Change talks, this involves practicing the conversational models in your mind, while at the same time visualizing how you and they might feel.

By visualizing the conversation before it happens, with emotional content, your brain's capacity for self-regulation will increase. And when the real conversation occurs, you'll be better trained for emotional regulation.

Qortex Coaching Application

Practice a Collaborative Change talk by trying one of the models presented in this chapter. Pick one model first, but challenge yourself to try them all. And as always, journal the results.

#EQ2iQ: Children Can Handle Collaborative Change

Don't underestimate a child's capacity to have Collaborative Change talks. The mistake adults make is to "dumb" things down. It can come across as highly condescending. Don't expect them to respond like adults but do speak to them with the same respect. Give them the same opportunity to collaborate as you'd like yourself. You'll be pleasantly surprised.

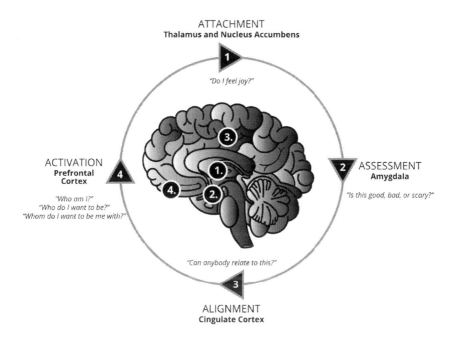

13
STAGE 4: ACTIVATION
ACTIVATE YOUR IDENTITY AND LEAD OTHERS WITH JOY

Activation is the final stage of the Qortex Circuit. It represents the highest level of executive function in the brain. It's also the final leg of the Team Qortex relay before the circuit completes and cycles back to stage one.

To fully activate stage four and become a Qortex coach, there needs to be a clear understanding between two ideas: self-esteem and self-concept.

Self-Esteem

In the 1990s, the self-esteem movement caught on like wildfire in North America. Seemingly every teacher, parent, and CEO wanted to believe that developing self-esteem could make people happier, improve performance, and even reduce societal iniquities such as crime, teen pregnancy, and pollution. The movement changed the development of an entire generation—the millennials. The truth was, however, real scientific evidence came nowhere close to validating all the hype around self-esteem.

To this day, many still believe that nurturing self-esteem should be the priority. The movement has evolved with the times and has many derivatives. One glance at the unending stream of positive "self-love" and "you're enough" messages on social media is enough confirmation.

Self-Concept

Self-esteem is generally the *feeling* we have about ourselves. It's the attitude we have towards who we think we are, which determines how we accept and approve of ourselves. In contrast, self-concept is the *knowledge* we have about ourselves. It's the self-awareness of how we think, what we enjoy, how we express temperament, our strengths, and our personal limitations.

Although self-esteem and self-concept are linked, there's a distinct difference between the two. Self-esteem occurs at stage two—assessment—of the Qortex Circuit, whereas self-concept is stage four—identity activation.

Self-Esteem vs. Self-Concept

Basing it solely on emotion can make self-esteem a highly subjective evaluation of self—based on what we believe to be good, bad, or scary. Therefore, self-esteem can become unrealistic because it can shift towards two possible extremes. The first extreme is that F.E.A.R. ("false expectations appearing real") can drive self-esteem, which results in labeling yourself a "loser" or "never lucky." The second is it can become overinflated, through mechanisms such as always winning medals for nothing other than participation, and distort your view of yourself. Regardless of the direction, the pursuit of self-esteem can lead to narcissism, unstable self-worth, anger, and sometimes violence towards those who threaten your pride.

Contrarily, self-concept is objective. Self-concept, however, doesn't mean we can't have emotions. What it does mean is that how we feel about ourselves is fully integrated with self-awareness. When self-concept is joy-based, we feel peace about our strengths and weakness. With joy, self-concept reinforces our identity even if we're feeling weak. With joy, self-concept reminds us that we belong even if we're feeling alienated or undeserving.

The other benefit of self-concept is self-compassion. Self-compassion is extending compassion to yourself in instances of perceived inadequacy, failure, or general suffering. In other words, when we're not happy with ourselves, we can give ourselves a break. We don't have to take ourselves so seriously; we can accept we're human. Self-compassion directly links to self-kindness, a sense of common humanity, mindfulness, and greater psychological health.

The stronger our self-concept, the more self-compassion we can have. While self-esteem is how we feel about ourselves, self-concept and self-compassion change the way we treat ourselves. Instead of being critical, pitying, or constantly comparing ourselves to others, we can be optimistic, curious, and develop resilience by reframing problems as challenges that lead to our personal growth.

The Prefrontal Cortex

Self-concept and stage four identity activation occur in the prefrontal cortex. The prefrontal cortex is located at the very front of your brain right behind your forehead.

The prefrontal cortex, considered the CEO of your brain, is most associated with executive function. Executive function relates to activities such as differentiating conflicting thoughts, making strategic judgments, predicting future outcomes, executing goals, and managing emotional reactions through impulse control. The prefrontal cortex also plays a major role in personality development and expression.

We're not born with stage four of the Qortex Circuit. The prefrontal cortex matures by the age of 25 (some say as late as 30). Stage four takes time and careful training to activate our identities and sense of belonging. And the health of stage four activation is highly dependent upon the foundation of stage three. But when fully developed, stage four of the Qortex Circuit represents the highest level of brain function.

Training the Brain for Stage Four Activation

By now, Team Qortex has completed three legs of the Qortex Circuit. As a review, when the race began, we developed appropriate attachments at stage one. Our brains asked, "Do I feel joy?" At stage two, we made appropriate assessments through self-regulation. The question was, "Is this good, bad, or scary?" Next was stage three, where we appropriately aligned ourselves and others. Here, our brains asked, "Can anybody relate?"

Finally, at stage four, the prefrontal cortex asks

- "Who am I?"
- "Who do I want to be?"
- "Whom do I want to be me with?"

The answers to these questions form ongoing narratives that combine for our self-concept. These narratives are the stories we tell ourselves and others, which in turn drive our behaviors. And the more our stories are based on joy, the more transformation becomes possible.

Transformation is a result of changing behaviors that are driven by self-concept narratives. It is different than using willpower for change. Willpower is a finite resource. If you've ever tried to break a bad habit by sheer determination, you know what I'm talking about. No amount of willpower can ever come close to a self-concept powered by identity, and a sense of belonging powered by joy. In other words, if you want to change your behavior, shift your self-concept to joy first—transformation will be inevitable.

When we can answer the questions, "Who am I?", "Who do I want to be?", and "Whom do I want to be me with?" with joy, we create what's called a generative image. Generative imaging is a skill that occurs at stage four of the Qortex Circuit.

Brain Training Exercise

The stories we tell ourselves and others define our reality. Generating imaging is how we put this principle to work for transformation.

A generative image is a picture that reveals the possibilities and potential for change. We can train our brains to create and access generative images continually. These generative images act as catalytic narratives to shift our self-concepts, change behaviors, and transform our realities.

Leaders use generative imaging to develop personal mission statements. My mission is, "Be a hero to my family." My mission is my generative image. I constantly visualize what being a hero to my family looks like in the past, present, and future. It's a generative image filled with joy, which is how to effectively maximize the potential of every generative image.

Oprah Winfrey's mission is "To be a teacher. And to be known for inspiring my students to be more than they thought they could be." Nobel Prize winner Malala Yousafzai has said, "I want to serve the people and I want every girl, every child, to be educated." Both missions create clear generative images and are prime examples of level four activation of the Qortex Circuit.

A generative image represents your ongoing story. Generative imaging is an iterative process that will continue to morph and adapt. Therefore, you shouldn't worry about crafting a perfect mission statement. It's more important that you get started. You can keep iterating as you go.

Start developing your generative image and mission with these steps:

Step 1: "Who am I?"

In a journal, answer the question, "Who am I?", and write whatever comes to mind. You'll start to engage your prefrontal cortex. Base your answers on what you know about yourself rather than how you feel (self-concept vs. self-esteem).

Step 2: "Who do I want to be?"

Start exploring a future vision for yourself. Base it on who you want to be versus what you want to do. Avoid making a bucket list. Also, avoid making emotional statements like, "I want to be happy," which is how you want to feel, not who you want to be.

Step 3: "Whom do I want to be me with?"

List the people you want to be part of your generative image and share your joy. Don't feel obligated to put any name. You'll know who should be on this list. This group is called your Qortex Circle.

Step 4: Generate the image.

Reflect on your answers. Then summarize everything into one or two statements that represent a generative image. Tweak it as you like. Make it as memorable and unique as you are. Remember, this doesn't have to be perfect. It's just meant to be a starting point.

Step 5: Share your generative image with your Qortex Circle.

Get your Qortex Circle together. Share your process and notes from steps one to three, then reveal your generative image. Tell them you're looking for encouragement and let them respond. If you've picked the right circle, they'll celebrate with you.

Qortex Coaching Application

Plan a regular meeting with your Qortex Circle. Keep the size of the group to three-way and four-way bonds. If more want to come, meet with them in different groups. Even encourage them to start their own.

Your Qortex Circle is not an accountability group. The purpose of the Qortex Circle is to be reminded of our generative images and share the stories of how they're progressing while maintaining joy. Practically speaking, it means Corrective Complex is strictly prohibited. Only encouragement and empathy are allowed.

Members of your Qortex Circle may not be as far along on the Qortex Circuit as you are. That's quite all right. Since you're a few steps ahead, you can coach them to catch up. It's the perfect excuse to become a Qortex coach!

#EQ2iQ: Generative Imaging for Children

In 1946, scientists started the British birth cohort studies and surveyed every woman in the UK that gave birth over one particular week. The study continued by surveying 70,000 children, at multiple points, as they moved through their lives over 70 years. The scientists studied factors that determined health, education, and overall thriving.

Dr. Helen Pearson pored through the data of the cohort studies and shared some key insights in her book *The Life Project*. Pearson writes a list of parental behaviors that the studies associated with positive outcomes for the 70,000 children, even those at risk. Here are the top three:

- Talking to and listening to your kids
- Making it clear you have ambitions for their future
- Being emotionally warm

This research provides a framework for parents and teachers to help children with generative imaging. Generative imaging for children involves having conversations with children about their future and listening with emotional intelligence.

Here are the steps:

- **Step 1:** Share how hopeful you are for their future and how much you believe in them.
- **Step 2:** Ask them what ideas or plans they have for their future.
- **Step 3:** Actively listen without entering Corrective Complex.
- **Step 4:** Suggest ideas to consider and ask them how you can be helpful.
- **Step 5:** Share your joy and thank them for collaborating with you.
- **Step 6:** Revisit the conversation regularly.

The more developed a child's prefrontal cortex, the more the activation center is stimulated for a cohesive identity. Make it an ongoing conversation, even as the child becomes a young adult.

14
ENCOURAGEMENT AND NEXT STEPS

Congratulations! You've completed the Qortex Circuit.

Before we continue, words can't express the gratitude I feel while writing (and rewriting) this last chapter. This book has been over four years in the making, and it's been a humbling experience. I want to express my sincerest thanks from the bottom of my heart.

Where do you go from here? I hope that you start coaching others sooner than later. It doesn't have to be in any official capacity unless you were already planning to become a professional coach. Whether as a manager, parent, teacher, or consultant, coaching can start with a small step as simple as sharing this book and working on it together. My point is, it doesn't matter where you start as long as you start.

Qortex Coaching

To get you started, I've included two appendix sections with additional information. The first section contains advice and different "hacks" for your own Qortex Circuit, which come from my experience coaching others. Use these tips and techniques to accelerate joy and transformation in your life. Then in the next section, you'll learn to coach others through a model I use with all my clients. But it's only meant to be an introduction to get you started. Qortex Coaching is a lifetime experience; we'll always be courageously learning and growing.

An Economic Vision

Remember, according to TalentSmart, individuals with high EQ make an average of $29,000 more per year. Knowing this, I envision coaching one million people to increase their EQ and make that kind of extra money. Achieving a vision like this would mean an extra $29 trillion in generated income. Now, what if every one of those million individuals were so grateful they donated a mere 10% of their increased earnings to social causes? That would be $2.9 billion in funding to change the world. Think about the economic and humanitarian boost that would be.

My heartfelt mission with the Qortex Circuit is to democratize access to EQ and social-emotional learning around the world. I believe joy and transformation are possible for everybody. This passion is the reason I unabashedly recruit coaches and develop tools to simplify the coaching process. If even a handful of us worked together at first, I truly believe we could eventually achieve the economic vision I see within our lifetimes.

Of course, I need to put my money where my mouth is. Let's continue this conversation! If you're interested, join me online by visiting www.edkang99.com or find me on social media @edkang99.

THE QORTEX CIRCUIT

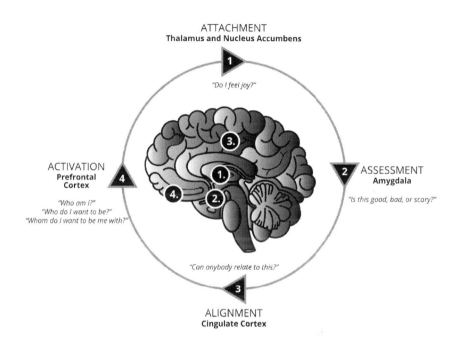

APPENDIX A
QORTEX HACKS

IN CASE OF RELAPSE BREAK GLASS

If you're using the Qortex Circuit to overcome serious habits or patterns, you'll find yourself relapsing in some way—most likely bingeing, which is completely normal. It happens to all of us.

The first step is to acknowledge that relapses are going to happen. Just accept there'll be setbacks. Visualize the guilt and shame you'll feel when you do relapse. Somewhere inside, you'll want to hide. Again, perfectly normal. You know those "in case of emergency, break glass" boxes? There's one for the Qortex Circuit too.

There's always a temptation to associate your relapse with your identity. Don't fall for it. You're not going to let one stumble on the Qortex track disqualify you from the whole race. A night of bingeing and self-debauchery isn't going to kill you or invalidate your generative image.

The secret is to reset the Qortex Circuit back to stage one. First, find someone you trust and gives you joy, and be vulnerable with your shame. Share how you feel and what you're thinking. Just have them listen. Corrective Complex from any source will only make it worse. If you do encounter Corrective Complex, run away as fast as you can.

Next is stage two. Do something courageous. Ask yourself, "What would courage look like right now?" Then start with the "Courage 3-2-1" technique and do whatever courage looks like immediately. Then plan a #10MCD.

Reflect on how you got to the point of relapse. Something was and might be still out of alignment. It might be a situation, relationship, or one of those unexpected curveballs life tends to throw at you. Figure out where the inappropriate alignment is and acknowledge it. You'll take care of this when the time is right.

Finally, get back to generative imaging. Remind yourself who you are. You're not the same person today as you were yesterday. Picture your mission. When you can, go share it with someone else and bring joy into their lives somehow. Do something kind for them. Be of service. Do whatever it takes to complete the Qortex Circuit and start the race over again by coaching someone else.

You got this.

BE THE JOY YOU NEED IN THE WORLD

Maximizing joy with the people may require being up-front with what you want and need from them. It's your responsibility to help them help you. The key is to do this without entering Corrective Complex. Use Collaborative Change talk models to do this.

Keep in mind that joy is caught not taught. Although you can teach people about Corrective Complex, so they don't sabotage their joy, joy itself is a relational experience. And it can only be experienced in the context of courage and vulnerability with strength and weakness.

Demanding joy from others is the epitome of Corrective Complex, especially if you're not willing to model joy for them first. But if you're willing to be the joy you need in the world, all your relationships will shift around you.

Test this for yourself.

STOP MAKING DECISIONS GOOD OR BAD
CELEBRATE THE COURAGE TO LEARN INSTEAD

Feeling scared when making decisions is a natural characteristic of the brain's assessment system. We're designed to assess the potential "good" and "bad" outcomes in everything. Any appropriate fear that causes us to pause can be healthy. Therefore, feelings of doubt can be appropriate as well. Doubt reminds us to double-check ourselves and make thorough evaluations. Doubt also motivates us to seek more information and improvement.

Decisions themselves, however—especially the results of those decisions—shouldn't be treated as good or bad. On the one hand, this type of thinking can lead to a lifetime of regret. On the other hand, we can become addicted to the "rush" of good decisions. Each presents a different challenge.

When we make a bad decision, it's tempting to wallow in the negative result. But if we see bad decisions as courageous opportunities to learn, then we can move forward without getting stuck. It's an approach that reduces the fear of taking risks, especially with similar situations in the future, because we can be optimistic that, regardless of the result, a valuable lesson is always on the horizon.

The rush of making a good decision can also get us stuck. The limbic system of the brain is designed to incentivize good decisions. After we make a good decision, the shot of dopamine our brain receives acts as a reward to motivate us to do more. Dopamine stimulates activities such as experiential learning and creative problem-solving. But the same reaction occurs when making decisions during activities such as gambling and investing in the stock market. Thus, when we get addicted to the rush of making a good decision, our emotional brains can override any rational decision-making process.

Instead of making decisions good or bad, celebrating the courage to learn from them is healthier for our Qortex Circuits. Assessing a good or bad decision is a Qortex stage two activity. The problem is that we can get stuck there. But treating decisions as courageous opportunities to learn, regardless of the result, moves us quickly to the next stage. By doing this, we'll never get stuck in either the rush of a good decision or the regret of a bad one.

WHEN YOUR QORTEX CIRCUIT IS FROZEN

The assessment center of the brain is commonly associated with the "fight-or-flight" stress response. When in danger, our brains choose between fighting or fleeing for our lives. But there's a third type of response, which is to freeze.

Freezing occurs when the brain tells our systems to pause while it decides between fight or flight. Physically, we may appear frozen, but in actuality, our minds are racing on overdrive and conserving resources for the next move. An example of this is the deer frozen in the headlights of an oncoming vehicle.

The freeze response can also lead to shutting down. Let's use the animal kingdom again as an example. Imagine a lion chasing an antelope. The antelope is in flight mode at first, but when caught, it goes completely limp. All systems in the antelope's body have shut down like sleep mode on a laptop. Triumphantly, the lion starts dragging its catch away for a feast. But for a split second, the lion gets distracted, and the antelope, who appeared to be playing dead, suddenly springs up and runs away.

We experience the same type of freezing, physically and emotionally. Physical freezing occurs with athletes that "choke" at critical moments during competition. It's as if their bodies abruptly forget the thousands of hours of practice and training. Choking occurs because the brain is pausing all systems to process the situation and determine the proper response to a stressful situation. It can happen right in the middle of a pitch, swing, shot, or pass. And it only takes a split second to disrupt an athlete's performance and cause a disaster.

Another way we freeze is an emotional shutdown. A traumatic experience can cause our systems to go "limp." Our brains are on pause to process intense emotions, which is our system's mechanism for self-preservation. It happens when our brains determine that there is no current option to fight or flee. The brain is desperately conserving resources, waiting for the right time to act.

The way to minimize the freeze response is to train the Qortex Circuit with simulation and visualization techniques. The first approach is to simulate stressful conditions. A professional sports team will practice and play preseason matches to simulate competitive conditions. Children also practice fire drills at school. Yet the results of these simulations can be mixed.

Over the past decade, there's been a steady increase in active-shooter drills in schools. The last thing we'd ever want is a student to freeze when threatened by an armed assailant. But while professionals assert these exercises can save lives, they also caution that these realistic simulations can contribute to depression and anxiety in the participants. Simulations are therefore only part of the solution.

Visualization is another technique that athletes use for mindset coaching. Visualizing an activity, such as shooting free throws in basketball, has an effect on the brain that is similar to really doing that activity. But visualizing the physical act is not enough. Emotions must be visualized as well to have the greatest benefit to the brain.

Emotional visualization trains the brain by creating neural pathways to help process a stressful situation and take appropriate action. It prevents any emotional shutdown from getting in the way of previous training. This technique starts with visualizing a stressful situation and the desired outcome. At the same time, it requires acknowledging all potential emotions and verbalizing them using "I feel" statements. Emotional visualization is, therefore, especially potent in situations where we need to hope for the best but plan for the worst.

Emotional visualization could be used to prepare students for an active-shooter drill while avoiding a mental shutdown. It's also useful for students with exam anxiety. And as mentioned, athletes can also greatly benefit.

The following is what you might say during an emotional visualization if you were a soccer player:

> I'm lined up for the penalty kick. I have a chance to score and win for our team. I can see the goalie and sense my team on the sidelines holding their breath. The entire stadium is quiet as well. I feel excited. But I also feel scared. I think, *What if I let the team down? What if this is my only chance to show my talent and make the national team?* I feel anxious about my entire future. There's so much pressure. Now I'm feeling nauseous. But I can't worry about that now. I'm going to live in the moment and trust my training. I hear the referee's whistle, and for a moment, my heart stops. I can feel the adrenaline and my heartbeat spike. I gather myself. I pick my spot and aim. I breathe and relax. I step in and make the kick. I score!

The more vivid the emotional visualization is, the more constructive an impact it has on the brain. What also helps is asking others to describe their own experiences in the same situation. Listening to a different perspective helps imagine any missing aspects or details. The key is always to process the worst-case scenario—the one that causes the most fear—until there's a sense of peace. This emotional preparation will take care of the freeze response.

VOLUNTARY HARDSHIP

Psychological resilience is the ability to mentally and emotionally cope with a crisis or "bounce back" quickly. A characteristic of resilience is "grit," which is passion and perseverance for long-term and meaningful goals. Resilience and grit create perseverance. Resilience and grit help us "stick with it" and continue working in the face of resistance, even after experiencing failure.

Individuals with resilient and gritty Qortex Circuits are unstoppable. But the question is, how do we develop these traits?

The answer is "voluntary hardship."

Voluntary hardship is the act of adding slightly-less-enjoyable routines to your life in small increments. It involves choosing growth over comfort by placing mini adversities in your path. The result is increased gratitude for life while fortifying your willpower and character.

Hellen Keller was an American author, political activist, and lecturer. She's the first deaf-blind person to earn a Bachelor of Arts degree, and became a worldwide famous speaker and author. In Helen Keller's essay "Three Days to See," she imagined what she would do if she had the ability of sight for three days. In the essay, she writes, "I have often thought it would be a blessing if each human being were stricken blind and deaf for a few days at some time during his early adult life. Darkness would make him more appreciative of sight; silence would teach him the joys of sound."

Voluntary hardship is not as trendy compared to other popular self-help advice. It's about discipline, delayed gratification, and embracing pain—voluntarily. It's certainly not sexy and doesn't make for very entertaining Instagram posts. But Hellen Keller understood something about resilience and grit that can benefit us all.

There are several ways to introduce voluntary hardship to train the Qortex Circuit. But whatever you choose must disrupt your comfortable routines in some way. Start with small inconveniences and then slowly increase hardship.

To begin, you could park in the farthest parking spot at the office and take the stairs. Next, start taking the bus to work one day a week, and instead of sitting on the bus, stand. You could also join a carpool. Finally, sell your car and buy a bicycle. The benefits will start to pile up.

Other voluntary hardships could be packing your lunches, making coffee without a machine, and forgoing condiments on food. You could also sleep on the floor, take cold showers, try regular fasting, or spend a day without your phone. To push the latter even further, you could downgrade your smartphone or get a "dumb phone" that only makes calls or texts.

(If you want to try something crazy, do a "dopamine fast." It's voluntary hardship on steroids that will reset your assessment center. Google it.)

To help you with voluntary hardship, train your brain to S.T.A.Y. ("stick to a yes"). When something is inconvenient and even irritating, close your eyes and say "yes" to the opportunity for voluntary hardship. Then S.T.A.Y. in that moment for a little longer.

For instance, imagine you're sitting in a park, writing in your Qortex journal, and a group of boisterous children start playing in the area. You're immediately distracted and somewhat irritated. It'd be easy enough to move. But instead, you take a deep breath, say "yes" to the voluntary hardship and S.T.A.Y for an extra ten minutes. You could try meditating or appreciating the experience, and then writing down your thoughts.

The best voluntary hardships are solo activities. Isolation and solitude amplify the benefits of any hardship. Being alone provides maximum opportunities for metacognitive reflection and self-awareness. Along with this, try not to tell people about your voluntary hardships. It's a principle based on the same reason we shouldn't talk to people about our goals. When we talk about our goals before completion, our brains start to think we've already achieved them, and we get demotivated. So, the same applies to voluntary hardship. Try to suffer in silence to ensure you S.T.A.Y. motivated.

The more we embrace voluntary hardships, the better prepared we are for the *involuntary* ones that always happen in life. Instead of panicking or lamenting life, you can count on your resilience and grit to carry you, and others, through any hardship.

TRY "WHAT IF" GENERATIVE IMAGING

One of the most powerful generative imaging techniques is to ask, "What if?" every chance you get. Doing this improves the generative imaging skill. The answers to asking, "What if?" can reframe realities for an instant transformation. Try reading the list below to see what they do for you.

"What if . . ."

- "I tried things a different way?"
- "I always said what I was really thinking?"
- "I forgave them?"
- "I gave myself a fresh start?"
- "I stopped taking myself so seriously?"
- "I just stopped pretending?"
- "I've found my real calling?"
- "I just served without expecting anything in return?"
- "I accepted their point of view without understanding it?"
- "I just gave them what they want?"
- "I just walked away?"
- "I questioned all my assumptions?"
- "I stopped eating sugar?"
- "I downsized everything?"
- "I took full responsibility?"
- "I'm supposed to be the leader?"
- "everything I want is not what I really need?"
- "I have everything I need already?"
- "everything I really want is just on the other side of fear?"
- "I only lived in the present moment?"
- "today is the day I'm finally ready to find my true self?"

IDENTITY POLTICS

"Identity politics" describes how people organize themselves and advocate for priorities along racial, religious, ethnic, sexual, social, cultural, or other lines. In identity politics, a group's specific promoted interests are narrower than those of broad-based political parties.

There's nothing wrong with identity politics as an approach for creating targeted advocacy. The issue is that identity politics can get us stuck on the Qortex Circuit.

For starters, politics in general tends to focus only on Corrective Complex. When a certain group's sole mission is to fix, convert, and direct with political power, there's no joy. For this very reason, political correctness can become incredibly toxic. Joy is the last thing on our minds when we're constantly afraid of offending certain groups that are incessantly trying to correct everything from our language to opinions based on political agendas.

What's more toxic is when identity politics only operates at stage two of the Qortex Circuit. Toxicity occurs when we judge specific identities as good, bad, or scary. What happens is labels such as "white privilege" and "toxic masculinity" are weaponized with shame and used solely to advance a political agenda, rather than start a conversation about equality. In this way, identity politics will always draw an ideological line between winners and losers, or allies and enemies.

I recognize this is a highly volatile topic because we're living in a time of culture war. So, let me use my own identity as a point of exploration.

I am Asian. Specifically, I am a Canadian born to Korean immigrant parents. (I also acknowledge that I am a cisgender heterosexual male, but we'll stick to being Asian for now.) Being Korean is part of my identity, but it isn't the only part. At stage four of the Qortex Circuit, my identity is prioritized by my spiritual beliefs first, then the responsibilities of being a husband and father. I also consider myself a leader and entrepreneur.

I've experienced racism multiple times in my life. I understand what it means to be judged by the color of my skin rather than the content of my character. I've been hurt and can only imagine what others that are more marginalized than me have gone through.

Thankfully, today I don't get offended by politically incorrect people. I have friends and associates who grossly misunderstand what being Asian means, and constantly treat me according to their stereotypes. I've never been offended by cultural appropriation. If others enjoy aspects of my culture to the point of making it their own, I appreciate their intention. And I didn't watch the movie *Crazy Rich Asians* because of the ethnicity of the cast. I watched it because I thought maybe I would enjoy it (I didn't). Most importantly, I've never called anybody a racist for disagreeing with my opinions as an Asian.

The last thing I want is to make my race a point of Corrective Complex and suck all the joy out of life. I'd only get stuck at stage one of the Qortex Circuit without joy. I'd also never make it past stage two because I'd be too busy judging others based on their good, bad, or scary identities. Instead, my goal is reaching stage three, which is to align people with empathy. And when I can relate to others, I'm ready for stage four.

At the activation stage, my brain functions at the highest executive level, and I lead others with joy—starting with my family. With my identity activation, I can have intellectual discourse and debates, even with those that have completely different beliefs. With my joyful self-concept, I can be open to new perspectives and collective sense-making without being threatened.

One thing I believe all people should agree on is the right to disagree and respect each other enough to work towards Collaborative Change.

Isn't Collaborative Change the original intent for politics anyway?

I'm not saying issues like racism and other forms of discrimination don't exist. I'm not invalidating the pain and injustice suffered by millions of oppressed individuals around the world. It's just that I don't believe the solution lies in arguing who's right or wrong and judging each other as good or bad. Transformation requires emotionally intelligent, agile, responsible, and mature dialog. As a society, we urgently need more joy.

I'll get off my soapbox (for now). But the point is to avoid making any identity good, bad, or scary. Don't fall into the black hole of today's identity politics. Instead, let's make our identities about the joy and transformation that comes through Collaborative Change. The possibilities for humanity could be endless.

@EDKANG99

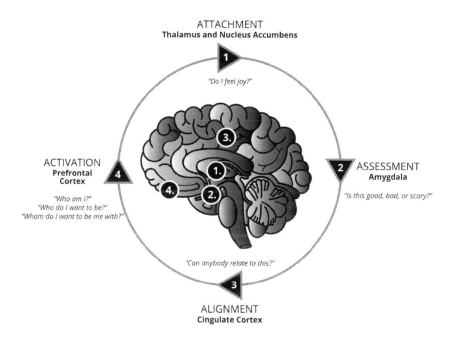

APPENDIX B
QORTEX COACHING

A MODEL FOR QORTEX COACHING

Whether you're a manager, parent, teacher, or consultant, you can become a Qortex coach.

Qortex coaching is broken down into three steps.

- **Step 1:** Identify where the Qortex Circuit is stuck.
- **Step 2:** Join their Hero's Journey to complete the Qortex Circuit.
- **Step 3:** Release to repeat.

This three-step process works in combination with any goal and any program. Whether it's sales training, starting a business or a health routine, tutoring, or online dating, the Qortex Circuit applies to it all.

Qualifications

Although they can be helpful, official coaching certifications or training are not necessary to be a Qortex coach. The only qualification is that your own Qortex Circuit is activated to stage four, and you're continually training your brain for joy and transformation.

Let me say this again with emphasis.

> *You can know all the right science, say the right things, and use the right techniques, but if your Qortex Circuit is not past stage four—identity activation—and your Team Qortex is not running with joy, you will fail miserably as a Qortex coach.*

Coaching Step 1: Identify where the Qortex Circuit is stuck.

The more familiar you are with your own Qortex Circuit, the easier it is to see where others are stuck with their own. To do this, you'll ask four questions for each stage of the Qortex Circuit.

- **Attachment Stage:** "Do they have joy in their lives?"
- **Assessment Stage:** "Is everything good, bad, or scary to them?"
- **Alignment Stage:** "Can they relate to others?"
- **Activation Stage:** "Who do they know they are, want to be, and want to be them with?"

Knowing where the Qortex Circuit is stuck will help determine where to focus your Qortex coaching. It'll also help you coach them through any resistance wired into the brain.

Coaching Step 2: Join their Hero's Journey to complete the Qortex Circuit.

There's a major distinction here between Qortex coaching and other types of coaching methods. In traditional coaching, the coach is the expert. And like a professional sports team, the expert stands on the sidelines during practice preparing the team to win.

The Qortex coach is different. Instead of standing on the sidelines during practice, the Qortex coach will get on the field and practice alongside everybody else. They're less like coaches and more like veterans that bring guidance and mentor the team. And when it's time to win, these guides are more than happy to get off the field and let the other athletes reach their full potential.

This difference is in the process of coaching. In traditional models, the coach is *apart* from the process, whereas the Qortex coach is *a part* of the process. Traditional coaches position themselves as experts. Qortex coaches are guides and mentors.

The Hero's Journey

Once again, the stories we tell ourselves, and each other, define our reality. In other words, narratives define everything for us. It's because the human brain operates on narratives. Narratives are the experiences we process and store as memories that contain emotion and information data. These narratives shape our personalities, guide decisions, and determine self-concept.

Our narrative nature attracts us to certain types of stories. These stories follow a similar pattern. There's always the main character that gets involved in an adventure, makes new friends, encounters challenges to fight an enemy, and through it, is transformed to fulfill their destiny. It's a pattern that is known as the "Hero's Journey," which is a term first coined in 1949 by Joseph Campbell.

The narrative pattern of the Hero's Journey is as old as time. Blockbuster movies today capitalize on it in different forms. From *Star Wars* to *Harry Potter*, to all superhero origin stories, and even the Bible, these patterns are ingrained into our cultural DNA. And again, it's because our brains are wired for them. Which means Qortex coaching synergizes perfectly with the Hero's Journey.

The Hero's Journey is broken down into multiple "acts." When combined with the Qortex Circuit, we can use the Hero's Journey to train every center of the brain.

1. **Attachment Stage:** Hero has a problem and loses joy.
2. **Assessment Stage:** Hero meets a mentor that knows the good, bad, and scary.
3. **Alignment Stage:** Hero forms allies and faces enemies.
4. **Activation Stage:** Hero embraces their identity for transformation.
5. **Attachment Stage:** Hero returns with joy.

If you haven't figured it out already, the coach is not the hero. The hero is the one who is coached, with the coach being the mentor. Your role as a Qortex Coach is to mentor the hero and help them tell and live a different story than the one that has them stuck.

Coaching Step 3: Release to repeat.

In every inspiring story, the hero eventually no longer needs the mentor, and the mentor knows when to let go. And in the best stories, the hero continues the legacy by mentoring the next generation. It's no different from Qortex Coaching.

The greatest achievement the Qortex coach strives for is to have those they have coached continue to go on and coach others. As a Qortex coach, your ultimate goal is to release your client to repeat the Qortex Circuit with others, which is a sign of true emotional maturity. In other words, work yourself out of a job as soon as you can. If you do, everybody's Qortex Circuit will be that much stronger.

#EQ2iQ: The Qortex Parent-As-Coach

Coaching your children poses unique challenges and requires additional consideration. The relational dynamics between parent and child must be managed carefully. But if approached with the proper wisdom, the parent-as-coach relationship can be quite rewarding.

Every parent starts with conditioning hardwired into their brains before they ever have children. We've all been conditioned to associate certain behaviors with positive and negative consequences through our parents, environments, and culture. In other words, we've been programmed by our stories to adopt norms and values that drive behavior. And more often than not, we're not even aware of it's happening.

These unconscious programs thwart the number one rule when using the Qortex Circuit for parenting: the child is the hero, not you, the parent. You're there to help the child identify and live their own unique story. They don't exist to help you continue yours. And until you become aware of the preprogramming that influences your parenting, you won't be a successful Qortex coach for your children.

I've offended my share of parents with this message. Some have walked out of coaching sessions. Others have accused me of trying to drive a wedge between them and their children. But I've seen enough broken families, teens struggling with addiction, alienated sons, bitter daughters, and concerned professional counselors to stand firm on my convictions.

The first step in becoming a Qortex parent is ensuring you are operating with self-awareness. Doing this requires getting unbiased feedback. It also requires mustering the courage to see what "you don't know you don't know" about your conditioning, and asking yourself tough questions such as

- "Do my children feel true joy when I parent them?"
- "Are they bonded with me by love or fear?"
- "How has my conditioning affected them?"
- "What story am I trying to tell?"

The bad news is, this is all hard work and can get ugly. The good news is the process becomes quite liberating. The best news is, it's never too late to start no matter how old you or your children are. And every parent's patience, vulnerability, and courage will always be rewarded.

QUICK REFERENCE COACHING GUIDE

To coach anybody, all that's needed is to present an example and follow a plan.

You're the example, and this book is the plan. To start coaching another, you can give them a copy of this book and treat it like a workbook. Go through each chapter together and share your stories. To help you out, whether you're the manager, parent, teacher, consultant, or actual coach, here's a guide.

Identifying Where They Are Stuck on the Qortex Circuit

First and foremost, stay out of Corrective Complex! Coaching starts with you and the state of your Qortex Circuit. Everything starts and ends with joy. When you've checked yourself for Corrective Complex, and everything's clear, proceed.

Stage 1: Attachment—Do they have joy in their lives?

Find out if the person you're coaching has appropriate people that they're glad to be with, in strength and weakness. If so, that's great. They should be encouraged to connect with them as much as possible. Most likely, the concept of joy, as it relates to the Qortex Circuit, will be new. Being stuck at stage one is common. You'll be the model for joy and what it means to be vulnerable in strength and weakness. Try to create three-way bonds as soon as possible, which may require introducing them to others you know. Or they might invite others to join their Hero's Journey, which could become group coaching.

Stage 2: Assessment—Is everything good, bad, or scary?

As you have conversations, if they describe everything using a spectrum of good and bad, while struggling with fear, they're stuck at stage two. If they're judgmental, then that is another indication. Practice the "Courage 3-2-1" technique with them and use cognitive inquiry to explore their F.E.A.R. narratives. Challenge them to act courageously regardless of what is good, bad, or scary.

Stage 3: Alignment—Can they relate to others?

Lack of trust, empathy, and social awkwardness are signs of being stuck in stage three. So are inappropriate relationships and broken boundaries. Coach them through the four levels of empathy and help them practice each. Challenge them to evaluate the relationships in their lives.

Stage 4: Activation—Who do they know they are, who do they want to be, and whom do they want to be them with?

Pay attention to the stories they share about their identity. How do they describe themselves? How do they talk about who they want to become? What is their identity concerning other people? Have conversations about reframing and embracing a new identity. If they've created a generative image, refer to it consistently. Help them with metacognitive reflection and generating imaging as needed.

Through every stage, monitor the conversations for Collaborative Change. Look for the emotion of courage and different levels of energy. Maintain joy.

Joining their Hero's Journey to Complete the Qortex Circuit

There's no one-size-fits-all Hero's Journey. Everybody's story is different. As the coach, your role is to mentor the hero through every stage of their story until it's time to release them.

Attachment Stage: Hero has a problem and loses joy.

Everybody who wants coaching starts with a problem. And every problem boils down to a relational issue. The key is to identify which relationships are being affected and where joy is lost. Coach them to tell this story and be vulnerable with their strengths and weaknesses.

Assessment Stage: Hero meets a mentor that knows the good, bad, and scary.

In every problem, there is good, bad, and scary. Share your experience and build confidence in a plan for how to navigate any F.E.A.R. with courage. Build trust and empathy. Always share joy. You'll be giving them hope that they can move past their F.E.A.R. into Collaborative Change. Remember, Collaborative Change means you're going to be courageous together, which means you should be sharing your F.E.A.R. as well.

Alignment Stage: Hero forms allies and faces enemies.

Every story has a protagonist, antagonist, and supporting characters. Listen to their stories for the entire cast, including those considered allies and enemies. There won't be bad guys like Darth Vader, Voldemort, or Thanos. But there may be inappropriate alignments that are getting the hero stuck. Have Collaborative Change talks to help them align their relationships.

Activation Stage: Hero embraces their identity for transformation.

Through the entire journey, the hero will constantly wrestle with their identity. But there's always a moment when the hero fully embraces who they are and becomes who they're meant to be. And although this shift seems like a sudden transformation, it always takes patience and time to get there. As a mentor, you can't force an identity or transformation. You can only help them process the emerging story until it all clicks. Use metacognitive inquiry and generative imaging to do this.

Attachment Stage: Hero returns with joy.

Every journey has an ending where the hero triumphantly returns home and brings joy to the people. The hero continues the legacy by mentoring others. That's when the mentor lets the hero go. But the relationship doesn't end. Instead of a coach-client relationship, a coach-to-coach peer partnership occurs as you each continue your stories.

Qortex Circle

The Hero's Journey is the perfect discussion material for a Qortex Circle. During a Qortex Circle meeting, allow everybody to share their generative images and update their stories on the Hero's Journey. Once everybody has had a chance to share, there can be open time for metacognitive reflection and inquiry. The group can also explore Collaborative Change together. And to sound like a broken record one more time: *No Corrective Complex!*

Manufactured by Amazon.ca
Bolton, ON